MAKING THE SHIFT

MAKING THE SHIFT

SHIFT

Becoming A Leader
Worth Following

Luke McKenna
UNLEASHING PERSONAL POTENTIAL

First Published in in Australia 2022
Copyright © 2022 by Luke McKenna

All rights reserved. Except as permitted under the Australian Copyright Act 1968, no part of the publication be reproduced, stored in a retrieval system, communicated or transmitted in any form or by any means - electronic, mechanical, photocopying, recording or otherwise without the prior written of the publisher.

Prepublication Data Servies available on request from the National Library of Australia

ISBN: 978-0-9943866-4-9 (PBK)

Edited by Kieran Blake
Typesetting and Design by Daniel Ojedokun

Published with the assistance of Lightning Source

TABLE OF CONTENTS

INTRODUCTION 1

PART 1: PERSONAL SHIFTS 9

PART 2: LEADERSHIP SHIFTS 55

PART 3: CREATING AN AUTHENTIC STUDENT LEADERSHIP DEVELOPMENT PROCESS 95

CONCLUDING REMARKS 125

ABOUT UNLEASHING PERSONAL POTENTIAL (UPP) AND THE AUTHOR 128

INTRODUCTION

WHY WRITE THIS BOOK

This short book outlines some of the most important shifts a person can make in their life. These shifts are explained from the experience of someone who has learned these shifts over time and continues to wrestle with them. While many of the shifts can be made in an instant, they need to be reaffirmed every day.

The main reason for writing this book is to help articulate and identify the shifts that can be made for a fruitful, healthy, prosperous life. The book combines lessons gleaned from 15 years of experience as a teacher, educator and leader, and clearly demonstrates the choices that are ours to make.

We see some pretty ordinary models of leadership in our world. We see politicians who make exaggerated promises simply to get elected, as well as greedy business leaders and sports stars who abuse their power. We see many people who are not aware of the personal and leadership shifts outlined in this book. And without that awareness, they don't have a very good chance of becoming a leader worth following.

Where are all the respectable role models for our kids?

Probably not in the headlines - they are busy growing themselves, serving, helping and leading their people. They are getting on with the cause. They are humble and don't self-promote. They put others first and we don't hear about them. This book is both an acknowledgement of those great leaders and a reminder to all of us that we should seek to emulate their behaviours, and not those we see in the headlines of our news feeds.

Why?

This book is written for educators - in particular for educators with their heart set on making a positive difference for their students. The objective of the book is to make students better versions of themselves. The students in our schools today will be industry leaders 20 years from now. For them to become better versions of themselves and better leaders of others, their teachers and school leaders need to understand and model many of the SHIFTS outlined in the pages of this book. As students and teachers make the shift, our schools will be better, and our families and communities will be better. As leaders make the shift, our organisations will be better and so will the world. It's the only way we can make the world a better place.

Where does it start?

It starts with you. Make the SHIFT and encourage others to do the same, because you cannot wait for the world to change in order to enjoy the benefits for yourself and others. When you change, the world around you will change as your influence expands.

> *"Never doubt that a small group of thoughtful committed individuals can change the world. In fact, it's the only thing that ever has."* - **Margaret Mead**

John Maxwell calls it the law of the lid. The lid represents the leader of any organisation and Maxwell explains that the people in the organisation can only rise to the level of the lid. In this way, no organisation can outperform its leader because the distance between the leader and the first follower is a constant. When a leader overperforms and stretches further, the team and followers overperform and stretch with them. When a leader underperforms, so do the followers. If you are a leader and you want your organisation to grow, you need to grow yourself first.

In the same way, great followers will not continue to follow if the leader doesn't grow. This book is for those leaders and future leaders in our world who want to grow themselves and the people around them. They want to grow not for economic gain, prestige or power- but for the benefit of the world, because great leaders make a positive difference in their communities and in the world. We need more of them.

True leadership also has a multiplying effect. Instead of adding our efforts, it multiplies our efforts because great leaders can recruit, select, inspire and guide other leaders to do the same, and this multiplies the effect of their actions.

DEFINITION OF A "SHIFT"

To shift means to move or cause to move from one place to another, especially over a small distance. A shift may refer to a slight change in direction, position or tendency.

Sometimes shifts might not be noticed at first. A change in direction can happen in a moment, but the effects of that shift are not obvious until some point in the future. This includes shifts in our mind. What we call a "mindshift" is a change of focus and perception which opens our mind to new ways of thinking and acting.

Take two planes as an example.

Two planes start at the same airport. One is travelling north, the other north-east. 3 minutes after take-off, they look like they're travelling on the same course and are only a couple of kilometres apart. Three hours later they both reach their destination, but the destinations might be 1000 km apart.

The planes demonstrate what a small shift, or a small change in direction, can do in our lives. Our life is the result of the small shifts, decisions and actions that accumulate over time.
Where you are right now in your life is a result of the shifts you have decided to make up to this point in your life. Where you are 10 years from now will be a result of the shifts you make over the next 10 years.

At UPP, our workshops with students are designed to shift people's thinking and even flip their thinking. The workshops aim to give students a new way because if they don't know of a new way, they succumb to what they have always done and do not get better.

As a dad, it's the same. I constantly try to give my kids the option of a better way of doing things.

As a leader of UPP, it's the same for our team members. We constantly share with our team that work is not just about making a career, but about service, contribution, impact, fulfillment and enjoyment. As a teacher, it's about helping students to understand that they have options and choices and that it is possible to choose the direction in which they want their life to go. These are some of the shifts in thinking that can change our lives.

Steven Covey said "you can choose your actions, but you can't choose the consequences of your actions".

We can also think about it as a choice between two pains. Yes, it doesn't sound like much of a choice, but we can choose between two unavoidable pains - the pain of discipline or the pain of regret.

For example - I slept in this morning. That extra 30 minutes was lovely and I avoided the pain of getting up and doing my workout. But all day since then, I've been feeling like I should do a workout. That's the pain of regret. I could have chosen the pain of discipline and forced myself to get up and exercise, but I chose temporary comfort for pain later in the day. Experience has taught me that the more I choose the pain of discipline, the better my life becomes. The pain of discipline hurts at the time, but we experience its benefits afterwards for longer.

Leaders help people understand that there is a better way. They help people understand the difference between the pain of discipline and regret, and the benefits of making small shifts every day. Leaders don't always have the answers, but they try to make themselves better with incremental improvements every day. Leaders know that subtle shifts over time and commitment to good habits over and over again make us improve, and they share this with others.

That is why leaders need to lead the way. They can't just speak the way, but must lead through their actions if they want to be believable as a leader, because if the leader won't make the shift for themselves, how can they help someone else to make the shift?
These ideas are simple to understand...but hard to execute.

THREE PARTS

Part 1 of this book examines PERSONAL SHIFTS. These are the attitudes, actions, mindsets and decisions we make that forge the direction of our personal lives and our connections with others. We cannot and should not lead anyone else until we can lead ourselves. If we don't make these shifts, we are not worthy of being followed. By making these shifts, we grow as people and increase our credibility as a leader. Once we have made these shifts, we will increase our personal effectiveness and become someone worthy of leading others.

Part 2 examines LEADERSHIP SHIFTS. These are the attitudes, actions, mindsets and decisions we make as leaders of people, and in our roles as leaders, that lead to the improvement or decline of our schools and organisations. The Leadershifts referred to in this book involve a paradigm shift that is required for us to be better leaders.

The final section (Part 3) of the book is about creating an AUTHENTIC STUDENT LEADERSHIP DEVELOPMENT PROCESS. You can consider the perspectives offered in this section along with the 10 action steps, and then use the audit tool to refine or develop the leadership process for your school.

MAKE THE PERSONAL SHIFTS FIRST, BEFORE THE LEADERSHIFTS

A good leader knows how to lead their team well, but a great leader knows the importance of leading themselves.

LEAD YOURSELF FIRST- You can't fake being a leader. If you have to tell someone you're a leader, you're probably not one. Leading others without the personal shift is shallow leadership. It's flaky, without substance and ineffective.

Are you worthy of being followed?

The following principles or laws guide our lives - whether we are aware of them or not. Live according to them and you will benefit. Ignore them and you will not. If you follow these principles, people will follow you, so be guided by them and experiment with the principles in your own daily life, and discover that people will let you guide them. The principles are like gravity; whether we believe in them or not, they continue to operate in our lives.

Leaders who don't first lead themselves may have positional power, but not influence.

The best leaders are influential and people want to follow them. A leader is a person who is aspiring to better themselves, and who cares about others. True leaders are rare. Leaders who truly lead themselves are hard to find, but if you've worked with one, you will know what I'm talking about. They help others to learn and grow, and are great human beings. They are not perfect, but they are intentional. They are worth following.

If a leader has no followers, they are not really leading - they're just going for a walk. Do you want to follow a person who is not aspiring to better themselves? Someone who doesn't care about others? Someone who is always complaining or blaming other people? I know I don't.

The best leaders that I have worked with all shared similar paradigms and world views, even though they were all different to each other. These traits and paradigms, which I refer to as personal shifts, are outlined in the following sections.

The following principles are some of the things I noticed about some of the best leaders I have worked with. They've made me aware of these principles (explicitly or implicitly) and I've tested them out.

They work every time, but sometimes I fail to use them well.

I hope that you can be aware of them. By raising your awareness of these guiding laws and principles, you will be a better human - someone who is very much worth following. An authentic leader.

PART

PERSONAL SHIFTS

From the inside out.

These personal shifts happen first. If you want to be a great leader who is worth following, you've got to lead yourself first. By making the shifts explained in Part 1 of this book, you will become a better human, and ultimately a better leader. Your life will be better, and you will be better able to love, serve, help and lead the people you care about at home and at work.

The personal shifts are as follows:

PERSONAL SHIFT #1- From reactive to proactive

PERSONAL SHIFT #2- From below the line to above the line

PERSONAL SHIFT #3- From circle of concern to circle of influence

PERSONAL SHIFT #4- From having to being

PERSONAL SHIFT #5- From playing a short game to playing a long game

PERSONAL SHIFT #6- From ordinary to extraordinary

PERSONAL SHIFT #7- From words to actions

PERSONAL SHIFT #8- From entitlement to gratitude

PERSONAL SHIFT #9- From me to we

PERSONAL SHIFT #10- From past and present self to future self

PERSONAL SHIFT #1

From reactive to proactive.

I've noticed that some people live by default. Other people live by design. To live by design means to live with purpose. To live by default is to live by accident and to just drift along without having any real purpose in life.

Do you want to live by default or by design?

The great thing is you can choose. You are in charge.

Being Proactive

Proactive people understand that they write the script by which they live.

> *"It's not about what happens to you, but how you respond to it that matters."* **Epictetus**

Proactive people have strong self-awareness and they use this to make the right choices in their daily lives. These choices can be big or small and they are what determine the direction that our life takes. Proactive people use their ability to stop, think and respond to any situation.

Choosing to choose.

Choosing to choose is the first and most important decision. At every moment we are faced with choices, and we must first realise that we choose to choose, or not. Proactive people will choose to choose, while reactive people will let choices be made for them, and they have less control over their lives.

I can complain about many things in life. I can complain or learn in the classroom. I can complain about my job, my colleagues or my boss. Or I can make the most of these situations.

I can criticise my work mates or teammates or family members, or I can support and encourage them. Making the choice to decide which action to take is not easy. However, even when it's not easy, we all still have the power to choose how we respond to situations, and to decide whether we will be proactive or reactive.

One reason that being proactive is difficult is that it requires thinking. Henry Ford tells us that "thinking is the hardest work, that's why so few people do it." Are you prepared to think? Are you prepared to be proactive and write the script of your life?

Being proactive improves our lives and the lives of the people around us. But what's the alternative?

Being Reactive

"Until we take responsibility for our lives, someone else runs our lives". **Orrin Woodward**

ZReactive people feel victimised and feel like they have no control. This is because in many situations they have given their power away by failing to choose or by waiting for someone or something else to make a decision for them. This is disempowering. I see many adults who think and live like this.

Reactive people use phrases like:
"There's nothing I can do", "I have to do this", "It's just the way I am".
This forces the person to think that the problem is "out there" and that the outcome of the situation is controlled by someone or something else. However, the real problem is thinking that the problem is "out there" and that we have no power in the situation. The more we think that, the less power and choice we have.

"We each build our own future. We are architects of our own future." **Appius Claudius Caecus**

"The best way to predict the future, is to create it." **Abraham Lincoln**

"All things are created twice." **Steven Covey**

Response-ability

Proactive people realise that they have responsibility. They take responsibility for the choices they make on a daily basis and don't pass this onto anyone else. Responsibility can also be thought of as our ability to respond, which is why we can call it 'response-ability'. When we relinquish our ability to respond, we give away all of our power and we live by default.

People think that the EVENT = OUTCOME.

However, the reality is that the EVENT + OUR RESPONSE (could be positive or negative) = OUTCOME.

Consider this scenario:

A friend uncharacteristically disrespects you and is rude to you.

How do you respond?

You could choose to respond by also being rude and disrespectful. This is likely to produce a negative outcome for you and your friend and to harm the friendship. In the same situation, you could think and respond with curiosity by asking your friend something like:

"Hey, you seem upset with me. Is everything OK?"

If you choose to respond in this way, your friend has the chance to share the problem and you can work together to solve it. The friendship with this person might actually strengthen because of the choice you made. It might not be easy, but choosing to respond this way is more likely to produce a better outcome.

This shows that it wasn't the EVENT that led to a positive or negative OUTCOME, it was the EVENT + OUR RESPONSE that led to the OUTCOME.

Things like this will happen in life. Our response determines if the outcome is ultimately positive or negative, and we choose this response because all of us have the power to choose. If we give away this power to choose, we live reactively and by default. Successful people are proactive and they realise that they get to choose, decide and design their lives.

Some people set intentions for their life each and every day. I encourage you today to set intentions and to take back the power to choose how you respond to situations, and to write the script for your life.

QUESTION TO CONSIDER:

Could you be more proactive in certain areas of your life?

PERSONAL SHIFT #2

Moving from below the line thinking and behaviour to above the line thinking and behaviour.

You can choose whether your behaviour is above the line, or below the line.

Below the line, we have BED.
BED = Blame, Excuses and Denial. This is the victim mentality. This is reactive. This is disempowering.

Above the line, we have OAR.
OAR = Ownership, Accountability and Responsibility. This is the victor mentality. This is proactive. This is empowering.

Many people in our world today choose below the line thinking and behaviour, usually without thinking too much about it!

They blame others for their problems. As Christopher Pike said:

> *"Whenever we point a finger at someone else, we simultaneously point three fingers back at ourselves."*

Blaming other people doesn't help because you can't control other peoples' behaviour, only how you respond.

So, what does it look like to behave above the line? It means, if you make a mistake, own it. Put your hand up and take responsibility for the problem and for the solution if you are capable of doing so. Get things done. Make it happen. The sooner you take responsibility and start working on a solution, the better your life will be. Fixing the problem is not easy, but the process is simple.

In contrast, staying below the line is easy. Anyone can do that. Even many adults operate below the line with their thoughts and actions.

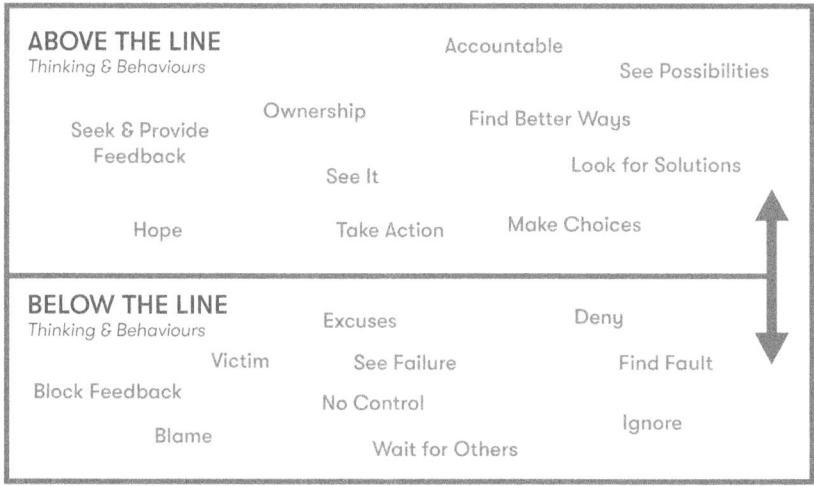

We all have a choice.

We can live below the line, with blame, excuses and denial, or we can live above the line and accept ownership, accountability and responsibility for our actions and our lives.

The window and the mirror

At UPP, we talk about passing praise out and down, which is an example of above the line behaviour. When your team succeeds, look at the people around you who helped create that success. While bad leaders look in the mirror and take all the credit for success, good leaders look "out the window" at others when things go well and share the credit for success.

Good leaders also need to look in the mirror. Not to take credit, but to reflect on what they could have done differently when things don't go well. They ask themselves what they could have done differently so that they can learn from mistakes and increase the chances of success in the future. Poor leaders look "out the window" at other people to pass the blame when things don't go well.

When do you look in the mirror? When do you look "out the window" at others?

Blaming others is common because it's easier. However, blame, excuses and denial don't ever fix a problem, but simply lead to more pain in the future. It is easier to live below the line in the short term, but the easy choice only leads to a lack of learning and growth in people.

Luckily, we are all free to choose. We are free to choose if we live above or below the line. We are not free from the consequences of our choices, however, and we see many examples in our daily lives. If we break a school rule, we receive a punishment. If we break a law, we pay a fine. If we take shortcuts in our work, people notice and the work is not of the same quality. In contrast, if we dedicate ourselves to sport, art, music or similar pursuits, we improve. We make the choice, and the consequence follows from that choice. We don't choose the outcome, but we are free to make the choice that leads to the outcome.

Above the line thinking and action can be harder in the moment, but it results in a better life.

Consider the following scenario:

Two people are experiencing financial difficulty.

Roger follows **below the line thinking**. He blames others, using excuses like bad investments, rising interest rates or a low paying job. People he talks to agree with him, because they're also living below the line. Roger and his friends are reactive. This is not empowering, and complaining instead of acting leaves Roger with the same problems 12 months later.

Paul uses **above the line thinking** to solve his financial problems. He takes ownership of the problem. Paul accepts that he is responsible for the situation he is in, and even though a bad investment has contributed to his problems, he is the one who can make it better or worse.

What does Paul do?
He seeks help. He talks to his bank about lower interest rates and makes changes to repaying loans he has with the bank. He works harder in order to add more value at work and receives a pay rise in the second half of the year. In addition, he spends less money on things he doesn't really need. After making himself accountable for the financial choices he makes for the next 12 months, he is then in a better financial situation than Roger.

It all started with the choice to live above the line.

Let's look forward 5 years from now. Where do you think Paul and Roger will end up?

QUESTION TO CONSIDER:

Where can your above the line thinking and actions develop further?

PERSONAL SHIFT #3

Changing from a focus on my Circle of Concern to focusing on my Circle of Influence

Another way to think about personal shifts is to think about our Circle of Influence and our Circle of Concern.

Circle of Influence

Our circle of influence contains everything in our life that we can affect, change or impact through our actions. Examples include our behaviour, asking for feedback, our effort, our dedication to studying and learning and how we treat other people.

Circle of Concern

Our circle of concern includes the things which affect us, which we cannot control, influence or change. Examples of things in our circle of concern include how other people behave, the weather and how well the other team plays a game of sport. It concerns us, but we can't change it.

It's true that we can't choose every part of our lives. We can't choose what the weather is going to be like this weekend, and that falls under the circle of concern. However, we can choose what we do on the weekend if the weather is rainy, windy or sunny. That is an example of acting within our circle of influence.

```
Someone Else's Decisions                         Death
How Others Treat Me         Others Taking Care of Themselves
Height                                      Who Likes Me
Skin Color                                Others Being Kind
             What I Can't Control          Who Loves Me
              What I Can Control
                 Doing my Homework
           Respecting Property    Being Kind
                  Being Accountable
                   Studying for Tests
               The Friends I Choose to Have
              My Decisions      Forgiving
              How I Respond to Challenges
          Trying Again      How I Spend My Free Time
             Doing My Chores   Taking Care of Myself
               Being Honest   Asking for Help
                How I Respond to Other
                      Apologising
Past Mistakes
Others Being Honest                 Others Apologising to Me
If Someone Else Keeps Trying                        Weather
Others Forgiving Me                  Others Asking for Help
```

Whatever we focus on expands. So, where do you put your focus?

If you put your focus on the things in the circle of influence, you can expand that over time. This is what proactive people do. If you focus on what you can influence, it will actually improve your life. We grow our skills, understanding, perspective and ability, and our circle of influence can expand.

If you choose to put your focus on your circle of concern, that will expand over time. This is what reactive people do. If you focus on what you can't influence, it doesn't usually help in your life.

If we try to control everything, and then worry about the things we can't control, we are setting ourselves up for a lifetime of misery and frustration. Unknown

Good leaders are proactive and they focus on their circle of influence.

Where do you spend your time and energy?

Think about your conversations with family and friends, and whether they are focussed on the things you can influence or the things you can't. Also consider what you spend your time thinking about, and how much of that time is spent complaining about things that are outside your circle of influence.

The more time you spend thinking about and working on things in your circle of influence, the more it will expand.

QUESTION TO CONSIDER:

Can I expand the time, energy, attention and focus that I give to my circle of influence?

Can I reduce the time, energy, attention and focus that I give to my circle of concern?

PERSONAL SHIFT #4

From "having" to "being"

"You've got to be before you can do and do before you can have." In short, you have to be a person of character and do the right things before you can have the things you really want.

The Art of Being, Doing & Having

- Who Must I **Be?**
- What Must I **Do?**
- So That I Can **Have**

To make the "be, do, have" theory valid, look at some examples in your own life, and do the following exercise on the next page:

1. Start with the right-hand column. List all the things you really want to HAVE in your life. This could be an education, good family relationships, a beautiful new home, a luxury car, a trip around the world, or to lose weight – you name it.

2. Next, work your way down the centre column. Identify the things that you must DO in order to HAVE the things listed in the right-hand column. As an example, let's say you want to HAVE a successful marriage. To do so, you must be willing to DO certain things, such as share openly, carry more than your share of the workload, encourage your partner, be supportive and make time for your partner.

3. Finally, go to the left-hand column and identify what you have to BE in order to DO so that you can HAVE. To have a successful marriage, some of the things that you must BE are faithful, attentive, caring, helpful, empathetic, encouraging, persistent, committed, kind, thoughtful and responsible.

BE	DO	HAVE

Now reflect on this process. You can use this basic formula for whatever it is you want to have.

Everyone wants to HAVE the stuff. Not everyone wants to DO the work or BE the person required to HAVE the things.

Jim Rohn says that "the greatest reward to becoming a millionaire is not the amount of money you earn. It's the kind of person you have to become, to become a millionaire in the first place." You need to BE the person and DO the things that allow you to HAVE what you want to have.

Look at what you have to do in order to accomplish your objectives, and then examine yourself and determine what kind of person you have to BE in order to DO so that you can HAVE. Most people try to achieve happiness in the opposite way. They focus on what they want to have, and not on what they need to DO or BE to HAVE it. You can't put the cart before the horse here - it's BE, DO, HAVE.

The Be, Do Have exercise above is adapted from Zig Ziglar's best-selling book Success for Dummies (Source: https://w5coaching.com/key-concepts-2/)

QUESTION TO CONSIDER:

How might you benefit by flipping your focus to being rather than having?

PERSONAL SHIFT #5

From playing a short game to playing a long game

Are you focussed on short term gains or long-term goals?

You might have heard the phrase:

It takes ten years to become an overnight success.

It means that some people might appear to achieve great success all of a sudden, but they did a lot of hard work and made the right choices for a long time before they enjoyed that success. We didn't see them making the right choices or working hard, because they were too busy working hard on their craft, and on themselves.

True leaders know that playing the long game leads to long-term excellence. Practicing is not amazing, studying is not amazing, showing up is not amazing, trying hard is not amazing, and often they're done alone and are not noticed. Only the results are noticed. That's why making the right choices every day and over a long period of time can lead to amazing results.

Playing the short game means chasing easy, immediate success.

Which way are you headed? What choices are you making? Are you getting better every day?

The best time to make the shift is right now. The best time to start acting on these questions is right now, because the sooner you put these ideas into practice, the better your life will be. It's never too late, as an old Chinese proverb tells us:

The best time to plant a tree is twenty years ago. The second-best time is now.

The best time to start making the shift is now.

No successful person has ever experienced accidental achievements. Even those who appear to be an overnight success spent a long time creating that success, because they made the decision to play the long game and to work hard and make the right choices every day. People who chase long term success gain great competence and this is honoured by others. Once they have achieved this competence, success and respect, they can become true leaders who act like leaders.

"Strength and growth come through continuous effort and struggle"- **Napoleon Hill**

"When opportunity presents itself, it's too late to prepare." - **John Wooden**

QUESTION TO CONSIDER:

What can you do each day to continue to improve yourself and prepare for long-term success?

PERSONAL SHIFT #6

From ordinary to extraordinary

We all have a choice. Our lives can be ordinary or extraordinary. What would you choose?

The beauty is that you can choose, and in every moment of your life you can choose to be proactive or reactive, and to operate below the line or above the line.

You can do just enough to get by. Teachers often call these students "cruisers". They do enough work so as not to make a problem, but never enough to actually produce anything great. In all walks of life, I see this. I see people who don't think about trying to give a little more, help a little more, learn a little more or do an extra set or rep, because they are happy to just get by. That behaviour will not set them apart.

I'm a believer that we can all be extraordinary at something. But unfortunately, most people fall short, because they don't intentionally seek it or work for it.

Dave Ramsey speaks about "excellence in the ordinary". It got me thinking about what this means for myself as a facilitator / leader / team member / father / husband. What does it mean for you in the different areas of your life?

Often when we think about excellence, we look for one giant step we can take to the next level. But, is there really one single thing that will help us progress? I think we should be very intentional about the choices we make, but that we should also recognise that our progress is a result of the aggregation of our choices.

If one can of coke made us unhealthy, no one would ever drink it. If one workout made us super fit, everyone would get out there and do it. But it doesn't work like that. These things take time. We build the habit...the result comes down the track.

I think we'd all like to be excellent, but how can we do it?

Excellence in the ordinary.

What does this mean as a facilitator or teacher who works with students?

It means doing the little things well. It means valuing ourselves and the contributions we make each day. We truly understand the impact of our actions on a daily basis, such as our attention to detail, respect for our colleagues, subject matter knowledge and preparation. We understand the importance of punctuality, constructive feedback, listening and smiling, as well as greeting students by name and making eye contact. We also understand the value of doing this with excellence.

It also means bringing the best version of ourselves - in our attitude and energy - every day. It involves seeking clarity and commitment in our communication with students, parents and our colleagues. Just as no one cleans up after the All Blacks, how do we leave the classroom or learning space at the end of the day, and do it with excellence?

Finding excellence in the ordinary means reminding ourselves that we are "white belts" seeking to master an art that can never be perfected.

In our relationships and personal lives

Can we give our children and spouses the attention and focus they need?

We can ask ourselves every day if we can really be present, and if we will put down our phones and be with the people we love. These things may feel mundane, and it's a battle to bring excellence every single day. In the words of Jim Rohn, wherever you are, be there.

We can challenge ourselves to listen for understanding and with excellence, and to strive for excellence in our relationships. Ask yourself if there is one thing you can do to be excellent in your relationships.

You may need to battle your own demons and thoughts, so you can turn up with excellence for the people you care about the most, and to ensure that you practice excellence for yourself, in your thoughts, self-talk, posture and attitude.

My future self is excellent - how do I live that now, every day?

To strive for excellence daily requires a strength of character. To strive for excellence in your health, your diet, your thoughts and your intellect is not easy, because it requires waking up when you don't feel like it, aligning your thoughts, filling your cup and striving to be the person you want to be.

They are very ordinary things, but they are a challenge. I'm not saying it's easy, but I'm saying it's worth it. This is excellence in the ordinary.

Sometimes...

We fall short. We mess it up. We eat junk food. We miss a day of exercise. At those times, how do we respond? How quickly do we get back on the horse? We are going to be weak, we are going to miss once, but the rule of thumb is to never miss twice.

What does this mean for the students we work with? Calling on our students to practice excellence means setting high and clear expectations for them, and acknowledging when the students are on track. It involves offering correction and guidance when they are off track so we can guide them back to the purpose, the learning and the message.

What about our student leaders? We must challenge them to rise by lifting others. We must challenge and support them to strive for excellence in their example, service and action. Excellence in their uniform and conduct, as well as their attitude, presentation and communication. Excellence not just in what they do, but in who they are being. We must call on them to respect and empower others through their leadership and remind them that they have been invited to serve others, and to do so with excellence. They should be encouraged to make the "Leadershifts" outlined in Part 2 of this book.

The challenge is not a small one. We'll mess it up often.

In order to progress, we don't need excellence in extraordinary things. Instead, we need excellence in ordinary things. It is not always easy to do, but it is important that we keep stretching ourselves to improve how we do the little things. That's excellence in the ordinary.

Habits of the extra mile
In our team at UPP, we seek to embody the habit of going the extra mile. Napoleon Hill describes this as the habit of rendering more service and better service than one is expected to render and doing it with a positive mental attitude. It's going above and beyond and blowing people away. Looking for ways to go the extra mile is how we become exceptional.

It's uncommon to go the extra mile. It's why we recently had this feedback from a school after we delivered one of our programs.

Please don't see this as a shameless plug for UPP- although I'm proud of what we do. It's just an example of extraordinary.

"It was absolutely incredible. I was blown away by the attention to detail, careful balancing of theory and practice, the carefully sequenced activities that built towards independence, the quality of the presenters, the workbook - everything. It was just so good, so impressive. Went way beyond what I expected. It was like you developed the ideal version of what I wanted the session to be, beyond what I thought could be included. So impressed. You all went above and beyond for this one." - Daniel Pozarik - Classroom Teacher - Randwick Public School, Sydney

We love feedback like this. But we receive it for two reasons.

Firstly, because we strive for it every day. We are intentional about going the extra mile. We make a choice that good enough isn't actually good enough. You've got to keep striving. If you're not growing, you're dying. Are you continually seeking improvement in the thing you want to be extraordinary in? We don't seek to be ordinary facilitators - anyone can do that. We seek to be exceptional.

The second reason we receive feedback like this is because it is very uncommon to be served at an extraordinary level. People are used to ordinary. But extraordinary is unique and different and it catches people by surprise. We are sure not to overpromise. In fact, we underpromise and seek to overdeliver. It works better that way. I would rather have feedback like this than have people ringing to complain - I couldn't sleep if myself or any of our team were doing work that was anything less than our very best. Could you?

How you do anything is how you do everything.

"Set your standards high, and keep them high, even if you think no one else is looking. Somebody out there will always notice, even if it's just you." - **Dianne Snedaker**

It's hard to do sloppy work one day, and great work the next. It's difficult to have a poor attitude in one area of your life, and a great attitude in another. When we switch tasks, our brain follows us. Our mindset and our attitude follow us. These things are more difficult to put down than a hammer or a whiteboard marker. They stick with us a little longer.

Someone who has a negative attitude, carries that attitude into any task. Someone with a positive attitude looks for solutions in any context. We can all remember people who look to drag other people down on the sporting field, in the classroom or even at home. We can also think of people who seek excellence in any environment.

"Your success in your career will be in direct proportion to what you do after you've done what you are expected to do." **Brian Tracy**

Exceeding expectations is fun. I want our team members to expect more of themselves than others do. It's fantastic when our team gets great feedback from a school, but they still discuss specific things they could do to make more of an impact next time.

How we do anything is how we do everything. It's true for you too.

These attitudes, mindsets and beliefs become habitual. We pick them up and take them with us without thinking too much about it. You would have heard the phrase that a certain behaviour was "out of character". That's because we come to expect people to act in certain ways. When people surprise us by their actions, we sometimes find ourselves re-evaluating that person in our mind. That's because generally how we do anything is how we do everything.

When a student lobs up late without their laptop to the teacher's first class of the year, the teacher doesn't normally expect great things from them in the second lesson. I'm not saying it's right that we extrapolate people's behaviour like that, but we tend to do it automatically.

Good leaders will hold their ideas of others lightly and be flexible with them, but they will also know that they need to ensure that their actions are in alignment with who they want to be and how they want to be perceived.

Those who are committed to their fitness plan do the sit ups when no one is watching. They also tend to get up early (of course we all have slip ups), work hard, invest in people. Because how we do anything is how we do everything.

> *"Your thoughts become your words. Your words become your actions. Your actions become your habits. Your habits become your character, and your character determines your destiny." -*
> **Lao Tze**

Leaders must realise that leading others involves helping and challenging people, being both warm and demanding, and doing so in order to help someone else get better.

QUESTION TO CONSIDER:

How can you focus on excellence in the ordinary each day?

How can you go the extra mile and maintain a positive mental attitude at work and at home?

PERSONAL SHIFT #7

From words to actions

When someone says one thing and does another, which one do you believe?

Aligning our words and actions

If I yell at my kids to be kind to each other (yep, I've actually done that), what does it teach them to do? At best it leads to confusion; at worst it has shown them that we yell at each other when we're frustrated.

When the leader of an organisation espouses certain values through a microphone or in an email, and then their actions don't line up, what does that do to their credibility as a person? What does that do to their credibility as a leader? Would you choose to follow that person?

When our actions and our words don't line up, we get ourselves tangled. As leaders, we lose credibility with people. No one wants to follow a fraud. Wherever possible, ensure your actions align with your words. If for some reason, you need to break your own rule, call it out and let your people know.

People tend to follow what they see. Mirror neurons in our brain mean that humans are good at emulating. You get back (from others and the world) what you give out. If you give out negativity, greed and harsh judgement - that's what you'll get back from the people around you. They will mirror it back to you.

Values and actions

I often see people hoping that words are stronger than actions in regards to organisational or school values. **Your values come from your heart and life first and then onto the wall or website, not the other way around.** You can't fake this stuff. Values on the wall or webpage mean nothing. Values in action make a difference.

The UPP values are Character, Excellence and Contribution. They come from how I live my life. They were formalised and made explicit about 5 years after we started UPP, although it's how we had always functioned. When we first wrote down our values, we used different words which essentially said the same sort of thing - we've become a little better at articulating them over time. I've had the opportunity to create something that I want to align with my life. Why would I pull it out of thin air?
I don't need to see values on the wall every day at work to remind myself to live them. It's just how I am, or at least how I strive to be. Many organisations create values first and they pay them lip service, but we articulate our values based on what we were already doing.

Articulating our UPP values clearly has been an important process too. It is also helpful because it scares away people who don't share those values. It attracts people that do share our values. If our values resonate with you, this is the best place to work. If they don't, it will be horrible, because we will always be challenging you on the values of Character, Excellence and Contribution. If you didn't like that, you wouldn't join UPP.

QUESTION TO CONSIDER:

What are your personal values that you strive to live by?

Are there certain values that you put into action a little more in your own life?

PERSONAL SHIFT #8

A shift from entitlement to gratitude

Gratitude changes things

Authentic leaders demonstrate gratitude and not entitlement. They shift from complaining about problems to being responsible for solutions. They look for solutions with situations, things and other people. They recognise that while they are the centre of *their* universe, they are not the centre of the universe.

On the other hand, some people are quick to condemn others and quick to complain. They are expert fault finders. The glass is always half empty with these people. They feel entitled to certain privileges and then are usually disappointed when they don't get them. Rather than give energy to the people around them, they tend to take energy away. What these people don't realise is that when you look for problems, you tend to find problems.

There is another way...we can train our brain.

Priming our brain with gratitude

Over time, gratitude trains our brains to scan our environment and focus on the positive. When we are looking for reasons to be grateful, we tend to find them. This happens mostly due to the reticular activating system (RAS) in our brain. Our RAS is like a filter for all of the input that our brain receives. Our brain is often overloaded with information and, therefore, it needs to make choices about what it allows into our consciousness. Essentially, our brain only allows things that are of interest or of threat to us to enter our consciousness.

Psychologists call this process of priming your brain to remain on the lookout for opportunities 'predictive encoding'. They have found that priming your brain to expect a favourable outcome actually encodes your brain to recognise the outcome when it arises (Siefert & Patalano 2001). It makes us about 3 times more likely to notice a positive. In the words of Henry David Thoreau, "It's not what you look at that matters – it's what you see."

Daily gratitude practice resulted in higher reported levels of positive states such as alertness, enthusiasm, determination, attentiveness and energy. In addition, gratitude correlates with goal attainment, high energy, positive moods, quality of sleep and more positive attitudes towards school and family (Emmons & McCullough 2003). Grateful people tend to bring joy to other people in their lives too. Other people enjoy the company of those who are grateful.

"He is a wise man who does not grieve for the things which he has not, but rejoices for those which he has." – **Epictetus**

"Give thanks in all circumstances." - **1 Thessalonians 5 (Biblica 2018).**

People who choose to be grateful wire themselves for more joy, opportunity and positivity. So, it is worthwhile to be a 'glass-half-full' sort of person.

QUESTION TO CONSIDER:

How can I regularly practice being more grateful for the situations and people in my life?

PERSONAL SHIFT #9

From me to we

Big Potential

Shawn Achor refers to our small potential as the success we can achieve on our own, while our big potential is the success we can achieve with others. Are you a big potential or a small potential sort of person?

Working well with other people is a great way to achieve more. When we recognise that other people have skills and experience that we don't, combining with others to achieve more seems like a great strategy.

While some people like to play their own game and keep to themselves, other people like to be part of a team. But we are social creatures.

The wisdom of the crowd

The wisdom of the crowd describes how the collective wisdom of a diverse group is usually superior to that of a single expert. In one such example, at a 1906 country fair in Plymouth, 800 people participated in a contest to estimate the weight of an ox. While the guesses varied greatly across the people in the contest, statistician Francis Galton observed that the median guess, 1207 pounds, was accurate within 1% of the true weight of 1198 pounds. We tend to do better together.

You will personally achieve more when you shift from a focus on me, to we. When you focus on helping others, and how they can achieve more, your life improves too.

Getting everything you want by helping others

The truth is, you can have everything you want - you just need to help enough people to get what they want. Be the first to give, or add value to other people when you can. Sowing always precedes reaping - so add value to others, provide service, help and support. Rather than being self-focussed, we should shift to being others-focussed. Great humans do this, and great leaders do this.

When you add value and do great work, you tend to get recognition and rewards. Doing good work helps people and it helps the world. By helping more people, by solving problems, by taking away pain, you make a contribution. In our lives, we are rewarded at the level that we contribute. Make a bigger contribution, earns a bigger reward. The contribution comes first, not the reward.

When you are young, work to learn. Don't worry about working to earn initially, as the earning will come later. If you learn a lot, contribute a lot and make a difference, the reward will come. There are no shortcuts to making a contribution.

In our lives, we first learn as students, then as practitioners, then as leaders. In reality, we are always students, because our skills grow as we help more people. We continue to learn more about ourselves and others through that process. In addition, we should always be figuring out a way to continue learning, growing and leading others and should avoid being content with where we are as a person at any moment. Always challenge yourself to learn and improve, and challenge yourself to contribute more, because the greater the contribution, the greater the reward.

When I started UPP in 2015, I was focussed primarily on myself and what I could achieve and how many students I could help. I then realised that I could work with about 10,000 students per year in person. There is a limit. That's my small potential. That's probably what I could achieve alone.

Since those early days, my focus has shifted to our awesome UPP team. I focus on helping our team members to get what they want. I serve them, support them, lead them. Their success is my success. When they have a big win, I can enjoy it with them. When they have a loss, we take the learning from that together. It's great to share the journey with these people. The more I help them, the more I get what I want. The better they are, the more people they can help.

At UPP, we have helped more than 250,000 students since we commenced operations in 2015. Last year, we helped more than 55,000 students with our exceptional workshops. We hope to eventually help 80,000+ Aussie students each year.

To have a genuinely positive impact on 80,000+ Aussie students each year, our organisation needs a better leader- I need to be better. I must grow myself, and in doing so, grow the people on our team.

Consider Personal Shift #4- from having to being... If UPP helps more than 80,000 students each year, I will HAVE plenty. But I need to BE that leader and DO the things required in order to HAVE a business that does that much good in the world.

In order to get the things we want in the world, we need to help more people.

Regardless of our line of work, the best way to become a billionaire is to help a billion people. The best way to become a leader is to help other people. To help other people, we need to make the shift from me to we.

QUESTION TO CONSIDER:

How can you tap into more of your big potential?

How can you provide more service, support and help to others in your life?

PERSONAL SHIFT #10

From past and present self to future self

Your future self

> *"Always make your future bigger than your past."* - **Dan Sullivan**

> *"Anyone who isn't embarrassed of who they were last year probably isn't learning enough."* - **Alain de Botton**

In psychology, "prospection" is the idea that whatever future you see for yourself is the thing that is driving your current behaviour. As humans, we are driven and drawn by whatever we imagine for our own future.

For example, if a teacher in a school setting sees themselves as a Principal (or in some other leadership role) at some stage in future, they will most likely be studying a Masters in educational leadership. What they see in their future drives the current behaviour.

If a young person wants to become a sports superstar, they will most likely be training long and hard to improve their skills. Whatever future we see for ourselves drives our behaviour now.

If someone does not see a good job or a bright future for themselves a few years from now, they will most likely not be doing anything to change that.

What you think about yourself determines the investment you will make in yourself. Our image of our future self is very important for determining the direction and trajectory of our life. I'm not saying we need to have it all worked out - of course plans change. But if you see a bright future for yourself, you are much more likely to live that future.

How do you achieve that future?

The key is to expand your vision of your future self. Think consciously every day about the vision of your life in the future and expand that vision. When we expand our life, we can do more, love more, be more, impact more. Whatever you focus on expands.

"Think about what you want today and you'll spend your time. Think about what you want in 3 years and you'll invest your time." James Clear

My future self is better than what I am right now. My future self is a better dad, leader, husband, coach and teacher. My future self will be better at doing all of those things in 5 years' time. My hope is that I will continue to develop my personal qualities. I will BE a better person. I will be able to DO more, and DO more effectively. It then follows that I will HAVE more. I hope to contribute more positively to the world.

Will you be a better person 5 years from now?

It's what you say to yourself, about yourself, when you're by yourself that matters. - Dr Benjamin Hardy

How do I do it?

Use these 5 journal prompts. Every 30 days, write down each question along with an answer. Doing so keeps you intentional, and also allows you to celebrate how far you've come.

Q1. Where am I right now?

Q2. What are my wins from the last 30 days?

Q3. What are the wins for the next 30 days?

Q4. What are my goals for the next 12 months?

Q5. Where would I like to be in my life, 3 years from now?

This process helps us to clarify and simplify our future. It also helps us to continue to expand and improve our future as we move closer to the goals.

Then ask yourself, how will you ensure you make your future bigger than your past?

How will you ensure that you are growing towards your 3-year goal? 12-month goal? 30-day goal?

> *"The ability of the average person could be doubled, if the situation demanded it."* - **Will Durant**

QUESTION TO CONSIDER:

What future do you see for yourself?

What are you doing now to move towards your best possible future self?

PART

LEADERSHIP SHIFTS

Authentic leadership

There is a great deal of cultural baggage regarding what good leadership looks like. In our society, many leaders might seem to be rich and powerful; decisive and strong willed; self-serving and narcissistic. Other leaders may seem to be level headed and calm in the face of adversity; all about helping their people; unselfish and kind. It can be quite confusing for a young person in our world who is attempting to find their way as they learn about leadership.

Many people are suspicious of those in leadership positions. Some people have been adversely affected by leaders. It's no wonder that many schools and organisations are struggling to find great leaders. Many excellent people do not aspire to be in positions of leadership. I believe that this is, in part, because many people have a distorted perception of leadership.

The following section includes many of the shifts in thinking about leadership - referred to as Leader shifts - that I have begun to make in my life. I have noticed that for me, the shifts have happened mentally at first, and have started to bear fruit in my life and leadership journey as I start putting them into practice.

The follow Leadershifts are documented in this section to bust prevalent myths about leadership.

LEADERSHIFT #1- From being served to serving others

LEADERSHIFT #2- From position and power to example and influence

LEADERSHIFT #3- From going up to giving up (high perks to high price)

LEADERSHIFT #4- From Win / Lose to Win / Win

LEADERSHIFT #5- From dragging others down to lifting others up

LEADERSHIFT #6- Uniformity to unity

LEADERSHIFT #7- Doing what you enjoy to doing what needs to be done

LEADERSHIFT #8- Tokenistic structures to genuine leadership roles

SHIFTS THAT BUST THE MYTHS ABOUT LEADERSHIP

LEADERSHIFT #1

From being served to serving others

Leaders have a role to play. Their role is to serve their people and organisation.

Serving others

Good leaders promote excellence in their organisations and their people. They see their role as one of service and they support, challenge and lift people up so that they can grow and succeed.

Good leaders accept the responsibility of solving problems within an organisation. They are happy for people to confront problems and use their skills to solve them independently, but encourage people to pass those problems up if they can't be solved immediately. They do this by dealing with the complexity of a problem and making situations clearer through their wisdom, experience and attentiveness. Leaders assist their people by helping to carry those burdens and make the load lighter for the people they are leading.

At the same time, good leaders pass praise out and down. When the group succeeds, the leader makes sure everyone within the organisation is praised for their contribution. They also 'go into bat' for their people, and this includes reducing unnecessary demands and by supporting in such a way that each person can grow and step up to the next level. Leaders understand that as their people get better, they are able to do more, and the organisation as a whole improves. This in turn encourages the leader to grow and improve more themselves.

Being served

Some leaders think that because they are the leader, they should be served. Leaders like this want more from their people than they want for their people. They make demands of their people, without offering support. They pass on a challenge and a deadline without support or guidance, then they stomp their feet when deadlines are not met.

Fill the water bottles

When I went to high school, I got an early lesson in leadership. I was made captain of our school indoor soccer team. I asked our coach (a teacher) what I needed to do as the captain of the team. He explained that the water bottles needed to be filled up before every game and brought to the court. I asked him if there was anything else, but he said that's all that was required.

I thought he would say I had to do the coin toss with the referee, give the players an inspiring speech before each game, put people in positions, run out onto the court first and be audibly encouraging. But he didn't say any of that. I didn't think much of this whole "being the captain" thing at first.

On reflection, however, it was a very formative experience. It showed me that the leader serves others; they fill the water bottles. The role of the leader is to make the work of others easier. It is to equip others with what they need and bring out the best in others. If the leader isn't filling water bottles for other people, who are they there for? The leader has to serve those they are leading.

Why do captains run on the field first?

We see elite sports team captains run out onto the field first and be lifted above people's heads when their team wins the trophy. What we don't see is why they run out at the front of their team. Good leaders are prepared to do the hard work first. They go into the combat zone and will lead from the front line whenever needed. That's why team captains lead their team onto the field. They are leading into battle. Good leaders know their people and they know the work of their people. They are prepared to do the work that they are asking others to do. Usually they have done it before, for longer, and faced harder circumstances.

The team captain gets to training first, and they leave last. They call anyone on the team who didn't seem quite right at training or in a team meeting, just to check in. They offer encouragement first. They take the blame first. If something is not right, people look to the leaders. Leaders care about their people. Captains take the fall first when their team messes up. Alternatively, if they try to shirk responsibility, their team won't get behind them. Captains are accountable after a bad performance from the team.

The role of the team captain is to lead, support, inspire and represent the members of their appointed team fairly and consistently at all times. They are not there to be served by the team, but rather to serve the team, even when times are tough. When your team is getting belted by the opposition, being the captain is not a perk. At these times the team is more likely to look to the leader for answers and for an example of how to react.

The captain is not necessarily the best player. They are, however, consistent and always play the game in the way that the team should play. They don't have to be the best player, because their job is to get the best out of every other member of the team.

In your work or general life, how can you lead by serving? It's a daily challenge and it can be a bit of a shift at first, if you're up for it. If someone on our team messes up, I am responsible as the leader. Our team knows that and I believe that takes the pressure off them.

In our context at UPP

Whenever a mistake is made in our organisation, first I think "how could we have prevented this?". "How could we have helped that person avoid that mistake?"

Sometimes it could have been prevented if I'd spoken to the person prior, if their coach was a little more proactive or if our system was better. These are things I can fix. When I own that, our team member feels supported and they know their leader is sharing the burden. As the leader, I share in the responsibility for their mistake. This also helps them not feel defensive or that their leader is going to throw them under the bus. Then I think about what they could have done to prevent it. I ask them what they learnt from the situation, how they might be able to fix it and how they could avoid a similar situation in future. Maybe they could have asked for clarity or support, been more prepared, or they may have needed extra training. Asking these questions helps us all learn and avoid similar problems in the future. Following this process also helps the team member grow and have a greater impact in future, and it helps me to be a better leader and create a better organisation.

From ladder finding and ladder climbing to ladder building

Throughout our working life, we tend to go through different stages. The stages are outlined here.
Ladder finding

We all go through a ladder finding stage in our working life, and this involves beginning our career and trying to work out what we should do with our life, and what skills we need to develop in order to achieve our goals. Sometimes, we might realise that we are climbing the wrong ladder, and we need to climb down and find a different ladder. An example might be switching university courses or changing career paths.

Ladder climbing,

Ladder climbing involves building those skills, knowledge and experience once we have chosen our path. During this phase we also seek to master our craft, so as teachers we become proficient in our classroom practice and also pursue personal excellence in our career. The focus is on growing ourselves, and it is a necessary step for all leaders. But it's not the end game.

Ladder holding

In this phase, we help others who might have fewer or similar skills and experience to us. We realise we can help others to be successful and that we can expand our influence. As teachers this can mean taking on a prac student, sharing best practice, mentoring young staff and focussing on helping others find and climb their own ladders. The focus turns from growing ourselves to serving other people as they seek to grow themselves. Even those who do not aspire to be in a position of leadership within a school or organisation should make the move from ladder climbing to ladder holding at some point.

Ladder extending

At this stage, the focus shifts to helping others to extend themselves. Our valued experience allows us to provide feedback as a critical friend, grow other people and move into leadership positions. In the educational environment, we might move into roles such as heads of department, pastoral leaders, literacy coaches or deputy principals. Our job is to help and extend key members on our team to help other people climb and extend.

Ladder building

When we reach this stage, we help other people build their own ladder. We give other leaders the skills, support and guidance to help other people ladder climb, ladder hold and ladder extend. This is real leadership. This is the stage of developing other leaders. It is the stage of serving our schools, organisations and communities by serving other people. In education, this is usually the work done by deputy principals and Principals.

It's not a race through the stages. Each stage serves a purpose. The best leaders are found at the stages of ladder extending and ladder building. At that stage, the focus is on other people and on helping the team to grow and develop. It is about coaching and supporting others to do the job well. It is also important to remember that the aim is to help other people be better at climbing the ladder than I am. How do I do that? By serving them.

Everyone is responsible for climbing their own ladder. However, leaders must be ready to set them up for success by giving them skills and by allowing people to experience non-fatal failure - the kind of failure which allows people to learn without dire negative consequences.

Note that ladder extenders and ladder builders are not responsible for doing the work of the person climbing the ladder. They are responsible for ensuring that each team member has the appropriate skills, experience and support to live and work with excellence. Nothing is more satisfying for a ladder builder than seeing a team member step up to a big challenge with great success.

In our context at UPP

On our team, we talk about milestones. Working with 50,000 students during your time with UPP is a significant "milestone" which four of our team members have surpassed. Another key milestone is the first time a team member is a senior facilitator on an UPP day. We are always preparing our people for that moment, knowing that "when opportunity arises, it's too late to prepare". When someone is a senior facilitator for the first time, it's a credit to that person for climbing the ladder. But it's also a credit to the people that held the ladder and extended the ladder for that person. At UPP, our ladder holders are called "coaches"- every team member has a coach (including me). Our ladder extenders are our Heads of the team, who support and guide the coaches.

The facilitators are the climbers. The coach serves the climber. The heads of team serve the coach. I serve the heads of team. When a facilitator wins, grows and steps up, we all win. Our ladder extenders and our ladder holders are constantly trying to help our ladder climbers be better at the work of facilitating exceptional workshops than they themselves are. We enjoy the success together, because we all helped that person grow. As we seek to master the craft, ladder climbing can be a thrill. When it is done well, ladder holding, ladder extending and ladder building is awesome.

That's what good leaders do.
If you want to be served, just keep climbing your own ladder and don't worry about anyone else. But if you want to be a leader, you better start getting used to helping and serving the people around you.

> **QUESTION TO CONSIDER:**
>
> Who are you filling the water bottles for today?
>
> Can you hold, extend or build a ladder for someone else to climb?

LEADERSHIFT #2

From position and power to example and influence

Some people think that leadership is about position. They think it's about the badge they wear.

My leadership story

In 2002, I had the opportunity and responsibility to be school captain. When the school Rector called me into his office and shared this news with me, I was delighted. I decided that I would do the best job I knew how to do. The trouble was, I had no idea what I was meant to do, but I gave it my best shot anyway.

Early in 2002, I was presented with a school captain badge at a very formal school assembly. I got a special College Captain pocket sewn onto my blazer. I gave speeches at important events, met with politicians and presented cheques to charities with donations that our school had raised. I did the best job I knew how to do as school captain that year. But now I know that none of that has anything to do with what it means to be a leader.

6 years after school, I met up with a mate for a coffee. I brought Laura (my wife) along, and he brought his girlfriend, who I hadn't met before. A few minutes into the conversation, my mate's girlfriend explained that she knew me, because her brother went to school with me. I assumed he must have been in my grade, but she explained that he wasn't in my grade, but was in Year 8 when I was in year 12. He had apparently told her that I was a really great guy!

Hearing this, I was pretty flattered and I thought back to my days at school, in particular when I was in year 12. As I was sitting there in the coffee shop, I wondered what I had done that made him feel like I was a great guy. I figured that her brother must have been very impressed with a speech I made as school captain, or that I'd inspired him to raise lots of money for a charity, or that he thought I looked great with the fancy blazer and badge that I paraded around the school in for the year. I figured I must have impressed him through being the "top dog" in the school.

So, I asked her "what did I do that made him say that?"
She replied "not much really...well, you used to say good morning to my brother."

Her response shocked me. I thought about all the impressive things I tried to do at school and the thing I get remembered for is saying good morning? How unimpressive.

I pushed her for more, as I realised there had to be more to it. She explained that when her brother started year 8, he hated school and he didn't find it easy. I happened to be one of the seniors in his home room class, and each day, I would greet him by name, with a smile. Some days, this was the only time a student outside of his year 8 class would acknowledge him. It made some days easier for him.

I know that it is a little thing, but to me it says a lot about leadership. I was remembered as a leader because I treated people well. The biggest impact I had on someone was not a speech, not a donation or meeting special people, it was greeting someone. You don't need a position, title or a badge to do it. Anyone can do it. You don't need to wait until sometime in the future. You can do it now. The biggest impact I had in year 12 had nothing to do with wearing a badge, it had everything to do with respect.

This is profound learning- good leadership is not about position or power. It's not about a badge - I don't actually know where that fancy badge is right now - probably gathering dust in the back shed. Leadership is about influence and we build this through respect, kindness, example and service, and through the connections we build with the people we lead.

I'm so lucky to have had that conversation 6 years after school in a coffee shop. It has helped me understand what leadership really is about and what it is not about. It has helped me commit to debunking myths about leadership, power, authority, position. At UPP, we now teach leadership to thousands of school students each year, who are reminded of the messages I've gained from that experience.

Leadership is something you do every day with the people around you. Anytime, anyplace.

What is influence?

Any time we influence the actions of another, we are a leader. John Maxwell tells us that "leadership is influence. Nothing more, nothing less."

Influence is...
- "to have an effect on the behaviour of someone or something"
- "the power to change or affect someone or something"
- "a person or thing that affects someone or something in an important way."

For our students, examples of being a positive influence may include: following the school / classroom rules - as this sets the right example for others; inviting others to join in conversations / games at lunchtimes; taking opportunities to help out fellow students or a teacher.

As adults in the workplace, being a positive influence may include: greeting people with a smile when you walk past them, focussing on personal excellence in any task which lifts the standards for the people around you, and going the extra mile to help someone on your team.

It doesn't require a badge, or a position. It requires influence. To paraphrase Margaret Thatcher, if you have to tell someone that you are a leader, you're probably not one. So how do we build influence?

We build our influence, firstly, by being aware of and trying to live out all of the personal shifts detailed in the first section of this book. Secondly, living out the ASPIRE framework, which is outlined in our leadership workshops for students- ACTION, SERVICE, PERSISTENCE, INFLUENCE, RESPECT, ENCOURAGEMENT. Good leaders and good team players do this, and it builds their influence.

What do real leaders look like?

In our work with schools, we often come up against a slight misconception from students about leadership. We also deal with misconceptions about who should be leaders. Many students seem to think that the leaders of the school must be the smartest students. They think that to be school captain you have to be good looking or smart or sporty or a goody two shoes or a great public speaker. They think that certain people have these attributes that make them right for the job.

In reality, good leaders are kind, supportive, courageous, fair, humble and positive. They are action-takers, service-oriented and empathetic. They ASPIRE. It's not about the speeches they make - especially if their actions don't back up what they are saying. It's not about any sort of campaign they run or speech they give in the week or day before nominations and voting occurs (yuk)! If your school promotes that, please read the rest of this book (especially Part 3 on Creating an Authentic Student Leadership Development Process) with an open mind.

So many people don't see themselves as leaders and so they leave themselves out of contention. I've played in sports teams where the quietest and most humble players off the pitch are the leaders on the pitch - through their actions.

True leaders do the work. They find what needs to be done and they help. They are involved and invested. They are committed to the team, group, school or organisation that they are leading. They probably love the group, organisation or industry in which they will be leading.

They are passionate, not perfect. Their passion is infectious and they're hungry to make a positive difference. They are inspiring because they are inspired to make something better, and people follow them because they have credibility. That usually comes from the fact that they are already leading by example.

QUESTION TO CONSIDER:

How can I build my influence for the good of others through my work or relationships?

LEADERSHIFT #3

From going up to giving up (high perks to high price)

The Perks
Everyone knows that leaders in most organisations have the big corner offices. They usually have larger pay packets, a car space and a fancy job title. Even in some schools, the Principals and Deputies often have these things. The perks are quite noteworthy and many people strive for those things. But any leader who has had their share of any of those things will tell you that along with the high perks comes a high price.

Nothing worth having comes easily or quickly. Leaders who focus on perks tend to love perks more than people, and are continually tempted to misuse people to receive, maintain or improve their perks. I'm a believer that doing this is short sighted, as anything led by a leader focussed on perks will come crashing down at some point. The choice to lead based on benefits does not benefit anyone.

"There is no success without sacrifice. If you succeed without sacrifice it is because someone has suffered before you. If you sacrifice without success, it is because someone will succeed after." - Adoniram Judson

The Price

The price that good leaders pay is what makes them better. The price requires you to reflect on your practice or on a conversation after it happened, and is what you must pay in order to be a good leader. In practical terms, it means long days, early mornings and late nights. It means biting your tongue at times and standing up to speak your mind at other times. Often, it's doing what is less comfortable. It also means studying a Masters level subject on your holidays, weeknights or weekends, skipping a party because there is work to be done and staying back after meetings.

I've noticed that we tend to notice the price that we pay personally. But we tend not to notice the price that others pay, or that they have previously paid. If someone is in a position of leadership, and didn't earn that position through nepotism or favouritism, you can be sure the leader has paid a price at some point. That doesn't necessarily mean that they are a good leader, it just means they have paid the price.

I have to give up, to go up, and I have to give up even more to stay up. - John Maxwell

The perks and price balance

There is no role in our career where we enjoy the perks without the price - the recognition without responsibility. While there have been times when I have probably received more or less credit than I deserved, it all levels out before too long. As soon as that balance tips too far towards perks or price, the pendulum will swing back the other way.

Good leaders must pay a price. But having paid a price is not enough to make someone a good leader.

Giving and taking

I lead because of what I can do for other people. But along my leadership journey, I made the shift from being focussed on what I can receive as a leader to what I can give as a leader.

Early in my career, I was climbing a ladder. I got into leadership because I was good with people and very hard working.

However, for a long time It was all about me. I felt that I needed the income and comforts that each new role would offer me. And to some extent, that is true. Starting a family, raising kids, buying a home are all expensive, and are worthwhile expenses.

At some point a few years ago, Laura and I realised that we had enough. We have more than we need for the financial security of our family. We've saved money for years and worked hard. We are fortunate to be in that situation in our lives. But I believe some people get to this point and keep accumulating. People get greedy. I'm not saying it's bad to earn good money - I think that's a blessing.

But the focus has to shift. From what I can get, to what I can give.

Now I'm interested in how I can bring more value to the people on our team. How can I help them grow and contribute more? How can they have a greater impact? Our team members know that they are rewarded at the level that they contribute. My job is to help them grow their contribution.

I concede that it is easier to focus on what you can give, rather than what you can get, once you have looked after yourself and your family. And it probably took me a little longer than most to realise that truth. But I think that the earlier we can focus on giving, the more there will be to give anyway. Start the practice of giving your time, treasures and talents now.

QUESTION TO CONSIDER:

Am I willing to pay the price that is required to grow as a leader?

How can I focus more on what I can give?

LEADERSHIFT #4

From Win / Lose to Win / Win

Symbiosis

Symbiosis is a close relationship between two species in which at least one species benefits. In human interactions, many people seem to think in binary terms. They think that for one team or person to win, the other must lose, and that if one person gets what they want, there must be a compromise (which in sporting terms would be a draw). But life is not like that. It is possible for 2 people or teams to come together and both walk away with a win. In fact, great leaders make this happen often. This is called mutualism.

Mutualism

Mutualism is a type of symbiotic relationship in which both species benefit. An example of mutualism involves goby fish and shrimp. The nearly-blind shrimp and the fish spend most of their time together. The shrimp maintains a burrow in the sand in which both the fish and shrimp live. When a predator comes near, the fish touches the shrimp with its tail as a warning. Then, both fish and shrimp retreat to the burrow until the predator is gone. The relationship gives the shrimp a warning of approaching danger, and the fish a safe retreat and a place to lay its eggs. Both species are in fact better off, because they coexist with the other species. This is a win-win. In our relationships, we should look for these win-win situations- where each person, group or team involved receives a benefit.

Win-Win or No Deal

Through UPP, we try to facilitate a win-win. Our workshops for students are an example of a 3-way win. A school tells us of a need and we offer a workshop to meet that need. The school and the students WIN and UPP WINS. In addition, our team members WIN, because they love doing this work and they get paid to do it. It's a 3-way or 4-way win.

Lots of people win in this scenario. It proves that one group/team/person does not have to lose in order for another group/team/person to win. In fact, for anyone to have a WIN, they need each other to have that WIN.

Many businesses operate in the same way, even the local supermarket. If a customer needs some milk, they go to the supermarket. They buy milk. The customer benefits from the milk. The supermarket benefits from the money. The staff at the supermarket benefit because they have a job, and so do the farmers.

We can apply the same principle to a relationship. If the relationship is not to the benefit of all parties, it will not be sustainable. When we hire people to work for UPP, we look for a fit. They might be awesome for UPP, but if we're not right for them based on the job demands or our company culture, it's not going to work. It's the same in any job. If someone really wants to work for us, but it's not the right fit, that's a WIN / LOSE. Even if they start working for us, and decide 3 months later that it's not the right fit and leave, all of the training and input is wasted and that changes from a WIN / LOSE to a LOSE / LOSE.

Ultimately, any deal should be a WIN / WIN, or NO DEAL. Anything other than a WIN / WIN deal will result in LOSE / LOSE at some point in the future. WIN / LOSE is not sustainable for the long term.

#ItsGoodToGive

Look for opportunities to give. Life has a funny way of giving to the givers and taking from the takers, so look for opportunities to give. Once a year, our team runs #ItsGoodToGive. During this fortnight, we pay our people an extra $10 - a very small sum. We ask them to buy a coffee / dessert or drink for someone else. It's good to give, and we should look for more opportunities to do so. The whole idea is to get our people thinking about opportunities to give.

During COVID-19, like many people, our family found ourselves in isolation for a week. To our surprise, one of our friends delivered a parcel full of fruit and vegetables for all of us and toys for the kids to enjoy in lockdown. The parcel would have been worth about $100, and would have taken considerable time to fill. As Laura and I reflected on such generosity, we know that this generosity will be coming back to our friends. They would feel great about it, but they can also take heart that they also have people in their lives (like us) that would do the same for them.

"For it is in giving that we receive." - **St Francis of Assisi**

QUESTION TO CONSIDER:

Where can you discover and create more win-win situations in your life?

LEADERSHIFT #5

From dragging others down to lifting others up

"Strong people don't put others down. They lift them up." - **Michael P Watson**

When someone in your workplace does something great or achieves a goal, how do you respond? You respond according to whether you feel challenged or threatened, or whether you feel confident in your own abilities. There is no need to be threatened by the success of someone else. Their success doesn't change you. Similarly, putting others down doesn't change your own position. Yet often we can be tempted to be a "drain" and not a "fountain".

> **Robert Ingersoll**- *"we rise by lifting others".*

This quote is very important to our team. We strive to serve and lift each other up. We believe that "a rising tide lifts all boats" and that it takes a quality person to lift the people around them. Lifting others is a better way to live.

A couple of years ago, I was talking with our Head of Team at UPP about two of our team members who he had worked with recently. We were talking about how we could help them take their next steps. We were also aware that a new opportunity would arise and were discussing which team member was ready for more of a challenge. Soon after, I chatted to one of the guys and he nominated the other member. When I asked the other guy, he told me how great the other one was. They were lifting each other up, not just with words, but with genuine respect and appreciation for the work they were doing. I understand that not all work environments are like this, because it's easier for people to pull others down to make themselves look higher.

You've probably noticed that whenever you give credit to others, it comes back around anyway. To be able to give a genuine compliment, you must have the competence, energy and courage to say something, and it therefore demonstrates that you are a person with the ability to notice others. Good leaders compliment others. They are generous and genuine with their praise and they feed into a culture of respect and lifting other people up.

QUESTION TO CONSIDER:

Can you find two people to give a genuine compliment to today?

LEADERSHIFT #6

From uniformity to unity

Some leaders essentially hire themselves. They hire people just like them because they are afraid of working with people who operate and think differently - afraid those people will highlight their weaknesses. Good leaders, however, hire people who compensate for their weaknesses, because good leaders thrive on the diverse skills and perspectives that different people bring.

In one of our student workshops, we discuss different leadership strengths. We help students understand that different people bring different skills, and that different skills can bring great value at certain times. No single skill is in itself more valuable than another, and no leader has every skill. Our skills can be developed over time as leaders, and great leaders understand their own strengths, as well as those of the people they work with.

In particular, we outline three different types of leaders - prophet leaders, planner leaders and people leaders:

Prophet leaders

These people are great at brainstorming and creating new ideas. They have a creative spirit and see the future with hope. They can communicate a vision with enthusiasm and energy. They are "light bulb" people who are imaginative and innovative. Their ideas can inspire others and make them feel excited. Not all of their ideas are great, but they will come up with many. However, they need the help of planner leaders to implement their ideas.

Planner leaders

These people are the organisers. They are practical and get things done. They like to plan and create lists - shopping lists, to-do lists and task lists. They delight in ticking things off as they are completed. They are detail-oriented and can usually spot a problem in advance, before it actually occurs. They consider who, what, when, where, and how questions. Planner leaders can become frustrated if things don't go to plan, as they usually spend a lot of time on the plan! They tend to get things done on time and do not like to waste time.

People leaders

People leaders are empathetic and caring. They are good listeners and seek to understand. Some people leaders are extroverted and like to socialise; while others are more introverted. They are not characterised by how much they mingle, rather by how much they care about others. People leaders give a voice to those who might sometimes be overlooked, and ensure all people are included. They are usually able to build meaningful friendships quickly and tend to have influence with people. People tend to follow people leaders.

It is important to realise that while we have three main types of leaders in this model, each individual person is really a mixture of all of them. No one has all of the skills. No one can do it all.
In fact, the best leaders know their own strengths, but are humble enough to call on the strengths of others. This gives other people the opportunity to take the lead at times and continue to develop their strengths. Good leaders understand the value of difference.

Most projects or events go through phases. To illustrate this point, let's use the example of a group of student leaders raising funds for a worthy cause.

First, the students will be tasked with raising a certain amount of money for the cause.

- Prophet leadership - They will brainstorm ideas for raising the funds, and ultimately choose the best ideas.

- Planner leadership - The next step is devising a plan on how to implement the ideas. This will include venue, promotion, creating a schedule, arranging equipment, staffing and many other factors. Then they put the plan in motion and organise the details.

- People leadership - Eventually, they will need to inform the community about the event, and ensure that the event or project team know their roles so that every participant enjoys themselves in the right spirit and benefits from the event.

In the very simple example above, you can see the 3 main parts of the project, and the three examples of leadership which are required to carry out the project. The three parts are interconnected, but good leaders identify each part of the project at any stage and call upon the people with the necessary skills.

To move from uniformity to unity, we need to recognise and celebrate these differences.

Laura and I think about things very differently. However, her perspective on everything at UPP- such as team members, schools, bookings, programs, research, marketing, revenue and wages, is hugely valuable. When I appreciate her perspective, I become a more expansive leader and I can bring more value. When I diminish her perspective, I limit myself and our organisation. In this case, two brains are better than one.

It's the same at many work meetings. If the leader doesn't take on the ideas and perspectives of others, they run the risk of losing perspective, relevance and connection with others. And in many cases, their decision making will be compromised and everyone loses.

Good leaders know their strengths, but they also recognise the strengths of others, and are not afraid to call on others at different times. Great leaders recognise that they don't need to do it all. In fact, they can't do it all - unless they don't want to achieve very much. Instead, by using the strengths of others, they give other people a chance to grow their skills, develop a stronger organisation and ultimately create a better outcome.

Achieving success doesn't require uniformity - it doesn't require everyone to be the same. Human beings are not the same as each other. However, we are equal, and we all have something to contribute. Success is borne from utilising the skills of prophet, planner and people leaders, and embracing diversity through leadership which creates unity.

QUESTION TO CONSIDER:

Where do my greatest strengths lie as a leader (prophet, planner, people)?

How can I better utilise the diversity of skills in the people around me, in a way that benefits our entire school or organisation?

LEADERSHIFT #7

From doing what you enjoy to doing what needs to be done

Good workers do what they enjoy doing. They do their job well. Good workers are usually able to apply their strengths in an area and develop them.

Great leaders and "impact players" don't just do the job they have or do what they enjoy, but find other ways to contribute. They focus not on themselves, but on the needs of the organisation, and they do what needs to be done. They find other ways to add value to the whole.

Great leaders do more than what is expected. They go above and beyond. They do a little extra once the job is done. They do it in a way that lifts the people around them. They find problems and tackle them, in order to offer solutions. They take initiative (without stepping on people's toes or undercutting other people) instead of just waiting for direction from someone else.

It is great to do what we enjoy. But sometimes, what needs to be done is not enjoyable, and it is the leader who should be the first one in to do the tough stuff.

In James Kerr's book, Legacy, he outlines how the All Blacks "sweep the sheds" after their games. In case you don't know, the All Blacks are New Zealand's rugby union team. They have a win rate of over 80%, have won many world cups and have been the best team in world rugby for the last 20 years. They have superstars in their team, but after every game they leave the dressing rooms clean. It is not their support staff who sweep the grass off the floor in the sheds and put the electrical tape in the bin; It is the players. In particular, it is their senior players. It may come as a surprise that this act of service is not delegated to the youngest players or to the debutant. The sweeping of the sheds is done by the most experienced and respected senior players on their team. They might have million-dollar contracts, but they are not too important to sweep the sheds. If there is a job that needs to be done, the genuine leaders do it.

If you want to progress in your career and life, take action when something needs to be done. Step up and lead at those times. Then, when things are going well, be humble enough to step back and share the success with others. This is what impact players do. This is what great leaders do.

QUESTION TO CONSIDER:

Where can I strive to add value by focussing on what needs to be done for the good of our family, school, community or organisation?

LEADERSHIFT #8

From tokenistic structures to genuine leadership roles

Coming up with an authentic leadership structure that fits the culture of your school is a considerable and important task.

If we create structures of leadership which tell students one thing through words, but demonstrate something different in action, this results in mixed messages and confusion.

Some schools give badges to everyone. They say that everyone is a leader. This works well in some contexts, but can prevent anyone from actually stepping up and leading. It can also be tokenistic and create a system in which the principals and teachers run the school, and just ask students to help as needed without input from the students. This can devalue the process.

On the other end of the continuum, some schools have SRC's where "every student is heard" and "we value student voice". This can also be effective, or can just result in many meetings and little action, and in a group of students with a badge but no genuine responsibility. Some students won't take this seriously, while others will focus on ways to improve some of the problematic aspects of school life, which can come across as fault finding.

In other contexts, we tell students that leadership is about service, but then we put on long lunches for them where they rub shoulders with VIPs inside and beyond the school gates. I'm not criticising, as it's very hard to get the structure right.

Before we examine the finer points of any student leadership structure, we need to look at the outcome we want to achieve.

I believe that most schools want genuine leadership roles that are focussed on service, contribution, and taking action on the needs of the community. If that is the outcome we are looking for, we need to move away from tokenistic leadership structures to genuine leadership roles.

QUESTION TO CONSIDER:

What are some ways to ensure tokenism is removed from our leadership development process?

NEXT STEPS

The following part of this book is the culmination of many of the ideas and shifts presented thus far. It outlines a process that attempts to breaks authentic student leadership development into parts. By doing so, we can investigate the parts and how they come together to make a cohesive whole. The outcome is an authentic student leadership development process that is relevant to the school context.

PART

CREATING AN AUTHENTIC STUDENT LEADERSHIP DEVELOPMENT PROCESS

After more than a decade of helping with student leadership development in hundreds of schools (through my work at UPP and through my prior experience as an Assistant Principal), I've had the unique experience of seeing many different school leadership development processes and structures. I've used this unique experience to develop an authentic student leadership development process that is educative, aspirational, transparent, positive and genuine.

Over the years, I have had many conversations with Principals, Heads of School and Deputy Principals about this topic, and about the process they have developed for their own school context. Many schools are doing great work with parts of their process, while other parts of their leadership development process make me cringe a little.

Striving for authenticity

For authentic student leadership development, the process and structure of leadership in the school is aligned with what the students are told about leadership. This results in buy-in from the community of stakeholders - students, staff and parents. On the other hand, an inauthentic process will be tokenistic and includes mixed messaging, campaigning and a popularity contest. An authentic process will look a little different in each school, but is based on the same core elements.

Do you notice any dissonance?

You may notice some dissonance between the intended messaging about leadership at your school, and the actual messaging portrayed by your leadership process and structure. The messages that most schools espouse are usually aligned to the leadershifts referred to in Part 2 of this book.

If our process and structure do not support the messaging or leadershifts that we are trying to convey, there will be dissonance. This dissonance can seem inauthentic. Instead of dissonance, we want to strive for congruence. When we have congruence, we have authenticity.

Where do you notice dissonance with your structure and process?

Once we have identified any dissonance, we can then seek to reduce this dissonance by aligning our process and structure with our messages. While we may not succeed in resolving all of it, we can reduce dissonance by being cognisant of it.

An authentic leadership development process will usually involve the following parts:

- **STUDENT LEADERSHIP DEVELOPMENT**
- **LEADERSHIP NOMINATION PROCESS**
- **LEADERSHIP SELECTION PROCESS**
- **THE ACTION OF LEADERSHIP**

THE 10 STEPS FOR AN AUTHENTIC STUDENT LEADERSHIP DEVELOPMENT PROCESS

The parts can then be broken down into the following steps...

1. Create genuine leadership development and opportunities to lead in informal ways.
2. Define what good leadership looks like with the whole cohort
3. Develop and communicate selection criteria
4. Share the leadership structure and roles with the whole cohort
5. Conduct a nomination process
6. Allow candidates to demonstrate competence
7. Voting / Preferencing / Endorsing
8. Selection Process / Assigning roles
9. Announce roles
10. Continued leadership development and taking action as a leader

STEP 1

PROVIDE GENUINE LEADERSHIP DEVELOPMENT FORMATION AND OPPORTUNITIES TO LEAD IN INFORMAL WAYS.

Can your students have a meaningful positive impact on your school community while developing their leadership skills prior to the commencement of the nomination process?

It is wise to provide students with multiple opportunities to lead with small projects that can contribute to the good of your school community. Doing so gives students the opportunity to develop their leadership skills without a badge or a formal title. In addition to developing their skills, it enhances student engagement and can create positive change in your school or local community.

Some ideas for student engagement and action

In primary schools, we may include a buddy system or bin, tuckshop, flag, litter or playground roster. Some schools invite students to be part of Student Action Teams, or volunteer to complete Acts of Service in small groups. In high schools, students could complete a Positive Impact Project that improves a situation or area of school or local community life. Some schools invite their students to "Go MAD- Go Make a Difference". This flips the focus for students - instead of thinking only about themselves, it helps students begin to realise that leadership is actually about other people. It's also about meeting a need and making a positive impact. Other terms that I have heard schools use include Service groups, committees, working parties and service teams. Notice that in each case, the focus is on how these students can give back and serve the community through meaningful action. These are just some of the strategies that schools use to give students an opportunity to lead through action, in informal ways, before they have the responsibility to lead in more formal ways.

If we have not genuinely sought to develop the skills of all of the students, it is likely that the students who show slightly more leadership potential will be selected into formal positions. Then, once they are selected, they will have further opportunities to develop their leadership skills and move further ahead of their peers in terms of leadership.

How can we ensure that leadership is not limited to only a few students in their final year of school? Can we create opportunities for students to be involved prior to the nomination process?

STEP 2

DEFINE WHAT GOOD LEADERSHIP LOOKS LIKE WITH THE WHOLE COHORT

Have students made LEADERSHIFTS? Do they know what makes a good leader and have they learned about and demonstrated the leadership traits that are outlined in this book?

At this stage, the school must ask itself if the whole cohort has had their concept of leadership challenged, changed and shifted, or if they still expect to vote for the goody two shoes, or the sporty, smart, or popular students.

If the school has not undertaken the formation process, the students who are vying for leadership positions, and the students voting, will not know exactly what is required of a good leader and students are likely to succumb to the existing myths around leadership. In addition, the candidates themselves might not know if they would make good leaders.

Instead, we should encourage our students to make the mental SHIFTS regarding leadership that are detailed in the first two sections of this book. The best way to do this is to book an UPP leadership workshop for your whole cohort and let our team bust some myths and start the conversation for your students.

This will align the cohort with the elements of true leadership. The next step is for the school to define the selection criteria for leadership.

STEP 3

DEVELOP AND COMMUNICATE SELECTION CRITERIA.

Is there a clear selection criterion that helps students understand the qualities of good leaders?

If we do not make a clear selection criterion for our students about what good leadership looks like, they will mentally create their own criteria. The voting stage then becomes a popularity contest. Without selection criteria, students may vote for the popular student, the good public speaker, the sporty kid, the goody two shoes, the smartest in the grade or the photogenic student who conforms to the criteria they created in their head. However, setting a clear selection criterion with every nominee and every voter helps inform the group about what is expected from a leader and what is meant by leadership.

Therefore, having completed a process of formation with students, you must create selection criteria for leadership positions. I believe this should involve two components - BE and DO. Typically, schools will include the DO part, but not the BE part. (For more background on this, refer to Personal Shift #4, in Part 1 of this book).

The DO part is like a CV or a resume - it includes things the student has done such as attending all sports carnivals, raising money for charity, attending the school musical and participating in two school sport teams.

The BE part refers to who they are BEING as a person. It relates to their character and personal qualities and includes how the student has behaved and how they have treated others. For example, do they set an example for others in the playground? Do they wear their uniform with pride? Are they a good influence on other people in the classroom?

Schools tend to miss the second part, which sustains the myth that leaders are students who are involved in extra-curricular activities and academics. While this tends to be the case, character is just as important. In this light, schools could use character strengths or incorporate some of the school's values in the criteria.

STEP 4

SHARE THE LEADERSHIP STRUCTURE AND ROLES WITH THE COHORT.

What is our leadership structure? What roles do we have? Are there genuine ways for students to contribute if they are not selected into formal positions of leadership? If the school has an SRC, does it serve a purpose?

In this step of the authentic student leadership development process, the school examines its leadership structure and looks at the existing roles. It also asks whether the leadership structure reflects the LEADERSHIFTS it wants the community to make, and if there are genuine ways for students to contribute if they are not selected for formal positions of leadership.

It's nice to give every student a badge, but this can actually make leadership seem tokenistic. We know that we are all leaders and we influence the actions of people around us without needing a badge. Therefore, giving tokenistic badges is the exact opposite of the intended message most schools are trying to espouse. Leadership is not something freely given to anyone who has made it to their final year of school, it is about service, responsibility, example and work.

Differentiate between all students who lead and those in formal positions of leadership

While all students should lead by example, service, influence, words and actions, some students also have a particular role. Therefore, it is worthwhile to make a distinction between all students who are considered to be leaders (usually the whole cohort), and those students who are in a formal position of leadership. Some terminology used to differentiate formal positions of leadership are Prefects, Captains, Student Representative Council and Leaders.

Leadership also carries specific responsibilities. Formal positions of leadership are usually tied to important areas of school life such as community, sport, culture, faith and justice, academics, environment, boarding, community service and house spirit - and each of these roles require work. If it doesn't require work, I suggest the role has become redundant. The students appointed to these formal leadership positions are required to set an example and influence others in a positive way (like everyone). However, they also need to do the work of leadership and complete projects that enhance an area of school life.

Leadership is not a reward; it is a responsibility. These roles are not bestowed upon students as a reward for their contribution. Instead, they are bestowed upon students because their previous contribution in that particular area has demonstrated that they would be able to carry the responsibility of that role.

Some schools model their leadership structure on the Australian Parliamentary system. They elect a Prime Minister and other Ministers. I quite like the term minister, as it has a strong link to service or providing something that is helpful to others. However, I don't believe that schools should model their leadership structure on the political structure in our country. Politicians are not the only leaders in the world, nor are they necessarily the best models of leadership for children. Very few people wish to move into politics, so there is no need to combine the two, and doing so could send mixed messages to students. If we need to teach a unit to Primary school children about the Australian parliamentary system, we can do that without making students think that all leaders are politicians!

Keep in mind, past performance tends to be the best predictor of future performance. I have seen many students really "turn it on" at the right time and make a late race for a leadership position. However, experience has also shown me that when students verbalise that they are ready to make a change or step up to leadership during the nomination or selection period, they are usually not. If they are ready, they won't need to tell you they are ready. As we discussed earlier in this book - if you have to tell people you are a leader, you are probably not one. Those individuals who are ready to lead will have already shown that they are ready, through their actions. This has implications right through the student leadership selection process, from nomination to assigning roles.

Are there genuine ways for students to contribute if they are not selected into formal positions of leadership?

Schools can give students genuine avenues to contribute even if they are not in formal leadership positions. Each school will likely find 20-30 active and very engaged students who have missed out on leadership positions, who can still contribute in a meaningful way.

In order to engage this group of students, find their areas of interest, and put them in a group to take real action on a project. Encourage them to join a positive impact project team on a cause that is close to their heart. For other ideas here, refer back to Step 1 of this process. They could also lead school tours for prospective parents, instead of getting the formal leaders (who are usually quite thinly stretched) to do everything. As we have already discussed, leadership is a team effort and the best leaders know that they are not the only ones with the necessary skills, knowledge and enthusiasm. So, let's model this to our students by giving genuine pathways for other keen and suitable students to be involved. The formal leaders can lead this group and utilise the skills of a strong group of enthusiastic supporters to make it happen.

Schools must ask if they can encourage their students to get involved and be great followers and supporters, and must give them genuine ways to do this.

Do we have a SRC (Student Representative Council), and if so, does it serve a purpose?

Many SRC's seem to be ineffective. Students are appointed into positions with no real focus or role, other than to share their views without any implementation. This model is often largely tokenistic, and the students display limited leadership development or impact.

However, if done well, I believe that they can be a good opportunity for leaders to listen to others and gain perspectives within their school community. They can then prioritise the issues raised and conduct further analysis for future action which makes a positive impact. Leaders are appointed to serve the community, so giving them a title and no scope to act is not really leadership and should probably be avoided.

Another potential weakness of a SRC is its composition. SRC's usually span over multiple year levels, and the same students can be given the leadership roles each year. Certain students have an opportunity to develop their leadership, while most other students do not have the same opportunity. This can lead to an unfair advantage for certain students, as well as the perception of favouritism as "it's always the same people who get the leadership roles".

I have also found that having the same students in SRC positions each year tends to disengage other students, who then show less interest in the SRC or leadership roles in the future. Therefore, if you have an effective SRC in action at your school, I would strongly advise preventing students from holding the position for more than one year at a time. Even though this might mean overlooking the strongest candidates in a particular year (who may have held SRC positions within a cohort the previous year), it ensures that the cohort continues to develop leadership capacity in other students, rather than just a small handful of students. This allows for the development of other students during the course of their school life, and recognises that all of our students are still developing their leadership skills.

STEP 5

THE NOMINATION PROCESS

In most schools, nomination time reveals 4 distinct groups of students within a cohort. Does your school have students in each of the following categories?

The first group comprises students who are suitable and enthusiastic candidates and who nominate themselves for a position of leadership.

The second group is hungry for leadership. They will knock down your door to nominate themselves for a position. Does this make them the best leaders? Is their motive to help others and serve the school or is it just to get the job/title/position? Sometimes those who are seeking leadership positions are doing it for the wrong reasons. These students will often miss out and then throw a tantrum. If that happens, you've probably made the right decision. They are enthusiastic, but not necessarily suitable.

The third group is usually quite obvious as well. These students are reluctant to nominate for leadership roles, and they would not be overly suitable for the roles (in fact, they may be quite unsuitable)!

However, there is a fourth group whom we may not notice. This is the mystery group, or the secret group. They are too humble to nominate themselves and they may need a little encouragement from a peer or teacher. Does this make them poor leaders? It depends. If they are disinterested and unwilling to serve the community, they should not proceed any further. However, if they are willing to serve the school community in any way that is helpful, they could be ideal candidates.

Is there a way that these students could be nominated by others?

If so, there should be a requirement for them to also accept the nomination, in order to show a willingness to serve. If these students miss out, they usually get on with it and lead anyway. They do it without a badge, behind the scenes or without expecting acknowledgement. These students don't like the limelight, but they might be quite suitable. They are humble contributors and in many organisations in the real world of work, these people get on with contributing at a higher level than is expected of them. Before long, they are given opportunities to be promoted into leadership positions because they tend to add more value, and people around them notice it.

Does your school allow for self-nomination, peer-nomination, teacher-nomination or a combination of these methods?

Furthermore, are we getting the highest quality applicants possible? Some schools (secondary schools in particular) struggle to find high quality candidates willing to apply. In certain cases, it is because there are a limited number of boys or girls putting their hands up. In other cases, it might be that schools tend to struggle to get strong applications for certain roles, year after year.

For which roles do students nominate?

Do your students nominate for one role only, or are they able to nominate for a range of roles? Some students would be wonderful leaders in many different roles. Some students may only want to lead in one particular role. I would have reservations about appointing a student to a senior leadership role (e.g., School Captain) if they are not willing to serve as a leader in another position. However, I believe that it would be very appropriate for some students to aspire only to other roles that do not include School Captain or Vice-Captain. I've heard of one school which required students to nominate for School Captain if they wished to be considered for any other role. I don't believe this is the best method.

STEP 6

DEMONSTRATION OF COMPETENCE

How do our students demonstrate their suitability to lead?

Most schools these days invite nominees to make a speech, especially for positions such as School Captain / Vice Captain. This seems commonplace now and is a reasonable way to go. However, it is not the only way to go and I don't believe it is the best way. For me, having students make a speech creates some dissonance. Schools should consider what is right for them.

Does a great 2-minute speech make you a great leader? Students could vote for leaders who say they do great things, or they could vote for those who have actually done great things. Talk is cheap. Actions speak louder than words.

Some schools encourage or allow students to make posters which promote their leadership campaign. That is how you become a politician, not a student leader. Consider how this form of campaigning would be received in the corporate world, and how colleagues would react if someone vying for a promotional position put posters all over the workplace!

I'm pretty sure that if I'd been asked to make a speech, I wouldn't have been School Captain. The Vice Captain that year was the state debating team captain, so if a speech was part of the selection process, I'm sure he would have received a standing ovation from any audience! As for me, I certainly would have been overlooked. Speech making is part of the job of the School Captain, but is it the only job, and is it all that's required to be a leader?

Instead of making a speech, candidates could take part in an interview. While this is helpful at preparing students for the real world, it is not necessarily a skill that demonstrates one's ability to lead. If we only interview candidates, the rest of the cohort don't receive the same interview practice. In terms of its validity for making selections, some students can present well in a 10-minute interview, but I'd argue that this does not make them a good leader, or ensure that they are one. I believe this is another example of combining two things which are individually sound, but not helpful when combined. Interview practice is good, but it doesn't necessarily need to be linked to leadership.

Some schools use a video submission. However, this is more likely to show someone's video editing skills than their leadership skills.

Other schools invite candidates to submit a portfolio. Again, this can show a student's ability to manage a project, be creative, follow instructions and meet a deadline. However, I once sat on an interview panel as an Assistant Principal and was fooled by a new graduate teacher who displayed their portfolio of work from their recent practicum experience. It all looked great in a portfolio, but the teacher did not perform well once in the classroom. Maybe we should have seen it coming. This proves to me that a portfolio does not demonstrate what someone can actually do.

If your school uses any of the above methods, maybe you have also been duped on occasion by a great presentation. This can be avoided.

One of my mantras with the UPP team is: don't tell me, show me.

Don't tell me you will serve and help others, just serve and help others.

If we ask students to tell us about what they are going to do, I believe it goes against the mantra that "we rise by lifting others". I'd rather someone spend time making a positive impact, not making a portfolio, video or speech to promote themselves.

Contrary to all of the ideas above, some schools only use the nomination form and the students' past performance when considering a leadership application.

Which leads to the question...

When do students really begin demonstrating their suitability to lead?

They say past performance is the best predictor of future performance. We can apply this principle to student leaders. Students who have attended a school for many years have had many opportunities to demonstrate their leadership qualities. They shouldn't be doing it all in the month leading up to the vote.

Students have had multiple interactions with their peers, teachers and the community, and have been involved in sports teams, musicals and the band, and may have even raised funds, participated in school life, encouraged others and volunteered. Some schools keep a database of student involvement in activities. If we refer back to Step 3 on developing a selection criterion that involves "being" and "doing", we may note that a database can be helpful for determining what a student has been "doing". However, a database doesn't necessarily determine how well they were doing it, or who they were "being" while they did it. That said, it can be a helpful tool, if a school has such records. Students who have participated in school life are the ones most likely to continue after the formal leadership positions are handed out, and leadership should be bestowed upon the students who have already demonstrated their willingness to get involved, serve, help and make things happen. It's too late to ramp up a campaign at the last minute.

I encourage all schools to consider when your students have actually begun to demonstrate their suitability to lead. I also believe that leaders should not be shameless self-promoters. However, in many schools, that's exactly what we ask students to do, in order to prove their suitability to lead! Go figure. That certainly creates some dissonance for me. If that's also the case for you, maybe we need to consider our leadership process.

STEP 7

VOTING / PREFERENCING / ENDORSING

How do we ensure that the voting process is not a popularity contest?

Are all voters equally informed about the selection criteria and also in their relationship to the candidates?

Firstly, let's consider who votes. If the people who are voting do not really know the candidates, why would we ask them to vote? If they don't really know if a candidate's words and actions line up, they are not informed. If they do not really have a clear idea of what it means to be a good leader, they are not informed.

If our voters are not informed, how much are their votes really worth? If uninformed people are voting, it is simply a perception management competition or a popularity contest which does not produce authentic leadership.

I imagine that advocates of student voice would be wrestling with the idea above as it might seem like some student voices are not valued. However, because we want students actively participating in the life of the school, and "collectively influencing outcomes by putting forward their views", their voice is very much valued. The school must ensure that the students are informed before they cast a vote.

It's no good selecting student leaders who are valued by staff and not by students. Student leaders need to lead the students, not the teachers. So, they need credibility and influence in the eyes of the students and must be setting a positive example for the students, as determined by the teachers. The student votes determine how influential a leader is and the staff votes more accurately determine the direction of that influence (whether it is positive or negative). Hence, staff and student voice are both valued. The students determine credibility, which can then inform the decision makers. The decision maker's job is to ensure that the influence and example set by student leaders is headed in the right direction.

There are two ways all voters should be informed:

1. They have an understanding of what it means to be a good leader. Students should not vote if they don't have this understanding.

2. They have journeyed with the candidates in order to determine character. This includes being in the same cohort and sharing experiences in class, sport, music, camps, socially and in other areas of school life.

We certainly do not want to disempower students by not giving them a voice. Instead, we want to give them an informed voice. That way, their opinions are more valid.

If other students (outside of the cohort who are being considered) are given the opportunity to indicate a preference as well, it would be wise to split the preferences. This could be done by separating votes from the same cohort and other cohorts. In this case, preferences from the same cohort should be weighted more heavily than cohorts below the candidates, as these students know the candidates better and are more likely to have witnessed their character as they have journeyed together for years (and are therefore better informed).

Another question to consider is whether all positions are subject to student preferencing or just the most senior roles like School Captain and Vice-Captain.

Do we use voting, preferencing or endorsing?

Voting is where students are able to vote for candidates. Normally, voting means that students can only vote for one or a certain number of candidates.

Preferencing involves students nominating preferences for their candidates in order (e.g., 3, 2, 1).

Endorsing allows students to support any number of candidates. Students can endorse all of the candidates they believe would be great leaders.

Collection of data is now usually done electronically (e.g., via google forms or survey monkey). This allows students to input their votes on their devices, and the reports can easily be created.

Schools should also consider whether any qualitative data is collected about candidates. In some schools, teachers are able to make a comment about candidates. These comments are not seen publicly but can be helpful for the selection panel. It is wise for the selection panel to seek counsel on the comments where necessary. They say that a picture is worth a thousand words... and I think that sometimes a few words can be worth a lot of votes (one way or another).

Does our school allow certain voters (teachers) to add comments about candidates?

Your school should choose which of the options above is right for you.

STEP 8

THE SELECTION PROCESS / ASSIGNING ROLES

This is the part of the process that tends to come under most scrutiny (from staff, students and parents), because at this stage the stakes get higher.

I suggest you effectively communicate an authentic process to all stakeholders so they know the steps involved in selection and the selection criteria.

Some of the key things that people want to know are:

How are roles assigned?

Are the votes of students and teachers all worth the same amount? Are the votes literally just tallied up and the roles assigned to the candidate with the most votes? In most cases, I'd suggest not. As such, it might be wise to call them preferences or endorsements, rather than votes. Or if we do call them votes, let's be transparent about the process. For example, it would be helpful for all involved to know that "the votes will be tallied up and then passed over to the College Leadership team for discernment before a final decision is made", or "the votes will be used as a guide to find the leading candidates. Once they have been determined, past performance and our selection criteria will be used to decide on leadership positions". Once again, in most schools, the data that has been gathered from the voting / preferencing / endorsing process is used by the panel to identify trends, and becomes part of the broader selection process. It is not simply that the highest number of votes wins.

Who selects the candidates for a position?

It could be one person or a panel. It is usually the responsibility of the Principal, along with the School Leadership Team or relevant middle leaders who form the panel. I would suggest not giving the responsibility for the final decision to any single staff member (unless it is the Principal), because this helps avoid the potential perception of favouritism.

Is it possible for students to be appointed into roles for which they did not nominate? For example, a student nominates to be House Captain and they miss out on that position. The selection panel then finds a subsequent position (Environment Captain) for which they would be suitable, for which they did not nominate. Is there a way that students are able to indicate on their nomination form that they are happy to serve in any position that would best serve the community?

It is wise to begin at the top. Start with the school leaders to ensure you have the best people for those jobs. Then move onto the other roles once the main whole-school roles have been appointed. There may be a tendency to have one student drop into another position because there is no other suitable candidate for that portfolio. However, I believe that slightly undermines the authenticity of the process.

In some schools, a larger group of leaders / prefects is chosen. Then, after further development or discernment, the school captains are selected from that group. There are situations where this is helpful, and other times where it is unhelpful, based on the roles available for leaders to fill. If, for example, a school elected 16 leaders, and then from that group of 16 two were to be selected to School Captain positions, that would normally be fine. However, it would not be fine if the other positions were house based and then it is possible that some houses would not have enough people in the final 16 to make that viable.

Your leadership structure will determine if this is right for your school or not.

STEP 9

ANNOUNCING ROLES

How do candidates find out if their application has been successful?

It is important that you inform unsuccessful students in a private and respectful way. It is normal for students to be disappointed. You could offer feedback to these students, however, allowing some time for students to process the decision before receiving the feedback is usually most appropriate.

It is also appropriate to encourage (or maybe even challenge) these students to support and lead in informal ways. These students will hopefully be the ones who are quick to support leadership initiatives in the school, so ensuring they are on board is important. If you have successfully carried out the process of educating them about leadership, there should be fewer issues at this "pointy end" of the process.

How do we announce the new leaders into their roles to the school community in both an educative and celebratory way?

Some schools announce their new school leaders with significant fanfare. These announcements can be tactful or over the top. We must bear in mind that leadership is a responsibility, not a reward. A tactful and educative way to announce new leaders is to have outgoing leaders pass on the responsibility, and you can do this in a number of different ways.

While it should be a great celebration for the community, it is also another opportunity to teach that student leadership is an accepted responsibility.

STEP 10

CONTINUED LEADERSHIP DEVELOPMENT AND TAKING ACTION AS A LEADER

Do we provide our school leaders with guidance, structure and support as they develop their leadership skills?

School Resources and handover

Is there a handover of wisdom and resources from the outgoing to the new leaders? Is there a staff member who can assist student leaders with particular roles? As well as having a student leadership coordinator, most schools assign a staff member as a mentor to each group of student leaders, based on their role in the school

Is there an electronic copy of speeches, position descriptions, previous projects, war cries and other resources that can be passed on to each new group of leaders? If your school does not have this resource in place yet, there is no better time than this year to start gathering this. It will benefit all of your future student leaders.

Leadership Training for your leaders

Do we provide our students with tools and further support to help them develop their skills and have a positive impact in the school community? If you do not currently provide this for your students, I would strongly suggest our Leading from The Front workshop, which helps develop the leadership skills of those students who are in formal leadership positions. Further to this, our Positive Impact Sessions are an online resource that you can use to help your students have a positive impact in your school community.

The first meeting sets the tone

If the first meeting of the group involves a long lunch with high-profile people, or a trip to a conference, what does this tell our students? Does it tell them that leaders receive perks, or does it remind the students that leadership is more about service and impact than it is about receiving benefits?

Reflecting and learning as a leader

Reflection is a key tool that all good leaders use. The school must allow leaders time for reflection throughout the year, so that they are able to learn from the journey of leadership. The most developed leaders tend to be self-aware, so we should provide our students with the opportunity to reflect on their challenges, their wins and their learning. Each time they lead a project, make a speech or run an assembly, they could be challenged to reflect on what worked well and what they might do differently next time. This creates the skill of self-reflection, which will make them better leaders and better people throughout their life and leadership journey.

Leaders are prepared to do extra work and usually show a willingness to learn. As a school, we should provide them with an opportunity to a) have a positive impact as a leader; and b) learn through the experiences as a leader.

Sometimes, students will need to learn from their mistakes. It can be difficult for teachers to watch this happen. We certainly don't want to set our students up for failure. However, it is possible for them to experience what we call "non-fatal failure". These are mistakes that they are able to learn from that do not have a detrimental effect on outcomes for them or the school community. Sometimes, the best lessons come from our mistakes.

School leaders are not a finished product. In Primary schools, they are 11 or 12 years old. In high schools, they usually are 16-18 years old. They, like all of us, are a work in progress and definitely have a lot to learn. I knew very little about leadership and what it meant to be a leader when I was a school leader. However, if our students can learn that this is just one step in their leadership journey, that is helpful. The truth is, they will likely have many opportunities to lead throughout their life. This is just a part of their leadership journey. Let's help them make the shift.

AUDITING TOOL FOR AN AUTHENTIC STUDENT LEADERSHIP DEVELOPMENT PROCESS

Does our student leadership development process align with the messages that we want our students to learn about leadership? Is there dissonance? The following questions will allow your school to conduct your own brief audit of your process, in order to seek improvements.

STUDENT LEADERSHIP DEVELOPMENT

STEP 1- Provide genuine leadership development formation and opportunities to lead in informal ways.
- Are there genuine ways that students can have a positive impact in your school community, while developing their leadership skills prior to the commencement of the nomination process?
- Do you have the opportunity to include Student Action Teams / Service Teams / Positive Impact Projects?

STEP 2- Define what good leadership looks like with the whole cohort
- Have the whole cohort had their concept of leadership challenged, changed and shifted?
- Do they just expect to vote for the sporty, smart, or popular students?

STEP 3- Develop and communicate a selection criterion
- Is there a clear selection criterion that helps students understand the qualities that good leaders have?
- Does our selection criteria include both DOING (what students have participated in or done) and BEING (how the students have behaved and how they treat others)?

- Have you communicated the selection criteria to students before the nomination process commences?

LEADERSHIP NOMINATION PROCESS
STEP 4- Share the leadership structure and roles with the whole cohort
- What is our leadership structure? What roles do we have?
- Are there genuine ways for students to contribute if they are not selected into formal positions of leadership?
- Do we have a SRC, and if we do, does it serve a purpose?

STEP 5- Nomination process
- Does your school allow for self-nomination, peer-nomination or teacher-nomination or a combination of these methods?
- Are we getting the highest quality applicants possible?
- Do your students nominate for one role only, or are they able to nominate for a range of roles?

STEP 6- Demonstration of competence
- How do our students really demonstrate their suitability to lead? (speech, interview, nomination form, video, portfolio, previous example)
- When do students really begin demonstrating their suitability to lead?

LEADERSHIP SELECTION PROCESS

STEP 7- Voting / Preferencing / Endorsing
- How do we ensure that the voting process is not a popularity contest? Are all voters equally informed about the selection criteria and also in their relationship to the candidates?
- Do we use voting, preferencing or endorsing?
- Are all votes worth the same amount, or are some votes

weighted? Are the votes of students and teachers all worth the same amount?
- Are all positions up for student preferencing or just the most senior roles like School Captain and Vice-Captain?
- Are we transparent about the weighting of votes?

STEP 8- Selection Process / Assigning roles
- How are our applications accessed?
- Are the votes literally just tallied up and then the person with the most votes wins?
- Is there one person or a panel responsible for selecting or appointing the candidates to a position?
- Do we use our selection criteria to assist the process of assessing applications?
- How are roles assigned? Is it possible for students to be appointed into roles for which they did not nominate? Is there a way that students would be able to indicate that they are happy to serve in any position that would best help the community?

STEP 9- Announcing roles
- How do candidates find out if their application has been successful or not?
- How do we announce the new leaders into their roles to the school community in both an educative and celebratory way?

THE ACTION OF LEADERSHIP

STEP 10- Continued leadership development and taking action as a leader
- How do we provide our school leaders with guidance, structure and support along the way as they develop their leadership skills?
- Is there a handover of wisdom and resources from the outgoing leaders to the incumbent leaders?

- How do we provide our students with tools and further support that helps them develop their skills and have a positive impact in the school community?
- Do we allow a time for reflection throughout the year for our student leaders, so that they are able to learn from the journey of leadership?

CONCLUDING REMARKS

I have a dream.

My hope is that all students and in particular, student leaders will have a formative experience of leadership. One that they will take with them throughout their lives, not just in terms of leadership skills, but also the paradigm shifts that we are able to provide within the structure of the school setting.

Imagine 20 years from now having leaders in business, politics, education, healthcare, media and across all sectors who want more for their people than from their people. Imagine leaders who are in positions of power and authority, with a focus on service and contribution, rather than greed and being served. Imagine leaders who care for people, the earth and our resources.

Imagine leaders who are looking for win-win solutions to big problems, rather than win-lose.

We have created some pretty big problems in our world, and it is the role of leaders now, and in future to help be part of the solution.

"We cannot solve our problems with the same thinking we used when we created them." **Albert Einstein.**

The Devil is in the Details – System Solutions for Equity, Excellence and Student Well-Being was written by Michael Fullan, along with co-author, Mary Jean Gallagher in 2020. In the book, Fullan and Gallagher make a startling prediction, that the human race is getting increasingly close to a tipping point that could go either way: toward flourishing or radical decline. Given the global events that have escalated since that time, it would seem to be very insightful.

The gap between the 'haves' and the 'have nots' is wider than ever and appears to be growing. "We have evolved to be extremely sensitive to social status. Bigger material differences create bigger social distances between us and add to feelings of superiority and inferiority. As people become more concerned with status, they become more out for themselves." (Wilkinson and Pickett, 2019)

Fullan and Gallagher argue, "We need a new moral imperative "to become better at learning and better at life". I also believe that we need to become better at leading.

In "The Devil is in the Details" Fullan and Gallagher observe that "the world is rapidly and increasingly becoming more troubled to the point that literacy, numeracy, high school graduation, and the like may be important foundational goals but are no longer nearly up to the challenges we face. Our students need these foundational goals; however, they also need much more.

Students need to consider how they can think globally and act locally. For our world to thrive, we need our students to become strong leaders who:
- are trustworthy, respectful, principled;
- care about people, the environment and the 17 sustainable development goals;
- will take positive action;
- seek to serve rather than be served;

- seek to unite, rather than divide;
- seek to contribute to people and the world around them, rather than focussing on greed and taking whatever they can get for themselves;
- who are mentally tough enough to handle the complex challenges ahead;
- seek to lift others up, rather than put others down.

This won't happen by magic. These skills need to be learned. These ways of thinking need to be taught. Students need the opportunity to practice these skills before they have the weight of the world on their shoulders. These are a few of the shifts that need to happen around the world, for our world to be better.

This book is my attempt to increase awareness of these personal shifts and leadershifts. By making these shifts, we will be better humans and better leaders, and we will be able to make our world a better place.

ABOUT UNLEASHING PERSONAL POTENTIAL (UPP)

At UPP, our mission is for every student to become the best they can be. Our vision is to impact 80,000 students each year to THRIVE as they LEARN, LIVE AND LEAD better, through exceptional workshops.

We deliver exceptional student workshops and camps; engaging, relevant, practical online lesson plans; and high quality professional development for teachers.

We seek to live and work by the values of excellence, character and contribution.

In 2022, we will impact more than 55,000 students to LEARN, LIVE AND LEAD better, through exceptional incursions. Since inception in 2015, the UPP team have positively impacted more than 250,000 students across Australia.

ABOUT THE AUTHOR

LUKE MCKENNA

UPP Founder and Director, Luke McKenna, is an educator and author who specialises in working with schools to help students learn, live and lead better. He has worked as a classroom teacher, middle school leader and Assistant Principal, before founding UPP in 2015. Luke has worked with educators and students across Australian primary and secondary schools from the independent, Catholic and public sectors.

He holds degrees in Business and Education, a Masters of Educational Leadership and a Professional Certificate in Positive Education.

Luke regularly speaks at conferences around Australia. His work has been published in the Australian Journal of Middle Schooling, Happy Schools and The Positive Times, and he is also the author of 'Thrive: Unlocking the truth about student performance' (2015) and "Making Wellbeing Practical- An effective guide to helping schools thrive" (2019).

Luke lives in Brisbane his wife Laura and their three gorgeous kids – Elijah, Oscar and Ava.

A NOTE OF GRATITUDE FROM THE AUTHOR

Eight years after beginning Unleashing Personal Potential, I am grateful.

I am grateful to have worked with some of Australia's best educators. I am inspired by their contribution, passion and desire to make the world a better place through education.

I'm grateful to be able to lead a team of passionate educators. Their positivity, humour and zest make this work so enjoyable.

Finally, I'm grateful to my beautiful wife, Laura and our three children. It is the greatest honour of my life to share the journey with you.

PRAISE FOR UNLEASHING PERSONAL POTENTIAL

At Unleashing Personal Potential (UPP), we work with schools who are serious about making a positive change and helping their students to learn, live and lead better. It is our honour to call them our partners.

Testimonials from some of our school partners are included below. For more testimonials from our school partners, please refer to http://www.unleashingpersonalpotential.com.au/

If you're serious about helping students learn, live and lead better, contact admin@unleashingpersonalpotential.com.au and we can discuss the best approach for UPP to work with your school.

PRIMARY SCHOOLS

"Amazing day and really engaging. Students and teachers really enjoyed it." Teacher- Coomera Rivers State School

"The best leadership program I have seen." Religious Education Leader, Our Lady of the Rosary, Kyneton, Melbourne.

"Yesterday was fantastic and Hogan was extraordinary. The students were very engaged and enthusiastic about what they learnt. I thought the structure of the day was very good. I'm glad I took the risk in trying something new. It paid off!" Teacher-

Ashburton Primary School

WOW! What a brilliant day! Pete had the kids attention and they were motivated and fully engaged all day. Thanks for such a great service. Principal- St Mary MacKillop Primary School, Keilor Downs

"Excellent day! Students engaged 100% of the time." Teacher- Musgrave Hill State School

"Fun, professional, very pertinent, accessible." Teacher- Mooloolaba State School

"We were very impressed with the day. The timing was perfect and the topics were very appropriate. The children enjoyed the day and related well to the presenters. We look forward to enjoying the experience at the same time next year" Teacher- MacKillop Catholic Primary, Birkdale

SECONDARY SCHOOLS

"Dynamic, powerful, engaging, relevant." Middle School Coordinator- Brigidine College, Indooroopilly

"Engaging, interesting and expertly managed session." Teacher- Mt Maria College

"UPP are highly professional in their approach, facilitating a leadership day with our College that uses theory and practical activities to engage and inspire our students to make an impact as College leaders in their senior year." Head of Students- Marist College, Ashgrove

"Fantastic. Excellent to see all students actively participating. Students were highly engaged and had a lot to take away."

Teacher- Toogoolawah State High School

"This presentation was excellent and very engaging. Had the right amount of humour. The stories from our presenters had a massive impact." House Dean- St Patrick's College, Shorncliffe

"We were extremely impressed with the presentation. The students were highly engaged and I felt that the session was a valuable one with a message that the students needed to hear. I don't think it would hurt for the whole school to hear a similar message delivered that well every term. A great presentation. I was in agreement with all points. It was one of the most significant moments of the year. Empathy, consideration, social skills, emotional intelligence. I loved it! He was a character I could relate to." Teacher- Lowood State High School

"Immediately took all of our students out of their comfort zone, challenging them physically, emotionally and intellectually. Presenters very quickly established great rapport and respect. Awesome." Year Coordinator- Yeppoon State High School

"An outstanding experience of leadership, through connection, activity, conversation, engagement and influence." Assistant Principal (Students)- Lourdes Hill College

"This is the best program I have seen in many years in this job. Well presented, energetic, meaningful with clear messages. Appropriate activities that allowed leadership and teamwork to be shown. Excellent." Head of House- Marist College, Ashgrove

"Fantastic day with a great message. All students should experience this." Teacher- Elanora State High School

THRIVE ONLINE LESSON MODULES

"The UPP online modules and lesson plans have made the teachers jobs easier, with resources and introductory activities that are not only engaging, but extremely relevant." Year Coordinator- Macgregor State High School

"The THRIVE resources are a wonderful introduction to vital concepts such as growth mindset, grit and wellbeing. The resources are easy to access and the teachers find them very dynamic and easy to interact with. The feedback from our students has also been extremely positive." Positive Education & Wellbeing Coordinator- Varsity College

TEACHER PROFESSIONAL DEVELOPMENT

"Best PD I've ever attended in 7 years of teaching. The entire day was useful. A fantastic presentation!" Teacher- St Clare's Primary School, Townsville.

"It was fantastic. Great ideas, practical, engaging. Great presenter." Head of Clan- The Springfield Anglican College

"A fantastic presentation that provides teachers with the tools to help students be the best they can be." Deputy Principal- Murrumba State Secondary College

"Thoroughly engaging and enlightening. Great presentation." Deputy Principal- Shailer Park State High School

"A clear, steamlined presentation with key topics that are very relevant to how we might start an action plan and change school culture." Deputy Principal- Burpengary State School

"Engaging presentation, all very relevant. Great use of analogies and examples for clarity. Activities were well placed throughout." Teacher- Brigidine College

"One of the best PD sessions that our whole staff have ever experienced." Principal, St Andrews Catholic School, Ferny Grove

"Well presented, informative, engaging sessions, which gave tangible actions to help deliver the content." Teacher- Coolum State High School

www.ingramcontent.com/pod-product-compliance
Lightning Source LLC
Chambersburg PA
CBHW070614010526
44118CB00012B/1515